WINGS

DISTINGUISHED STUDENT ESSAYS
22ND EDITION

From the First-Year Composition Program at California State University, Northridge

Editors: Melisa Malvin-Middleton and Emily Olson

Assistant Editors: Rachel Dulaney and Jennifer E. Lee

HAYDEN
HM
McNEIL

Hayden-McNeil Sustainability

Hayden-McNeil's standard paper stock uses a minimum of 30% post-consumer waste. We offer higher % options by request, including a 100% recycled stock. Additionally, Hayden-McNeil Custom Digital provides authors with the opportunity to convert print products to a digital format. Hayden-McNeil is part of a larger sustainability initiative through Macmillan Higher Ed. Visit http://sustainability.macmillan.com to learn more.

Printed in the United States of America

10 9 8 7 6 5 4 3 2 1

ISBN 978-0-7380-7885-4

Hayden-McNeil Publishing
14903 Pilot Drive
Plymouth, MI 48170
www.hmpublishing.com

ClarkI 7885-4 F15

TABLE OF CONTENTS

Letter from the Editors

We are proud to put forth this collection of first-year student writing from California State University, Northridge, in this, the 22nd edition of *Wings*. This collection represents the voices of your peers, who have faced the same challenges in their first-year writing courses that you find yourself experiencing. The authors of these pieces struggled to master the various writing assignments you will encounter, and as you will read in many of their author statements, they did not always succeed the first time. These emerging writers learned that writing is a process; they worked hard to arrive at the final product you will read here. Their writing processes involved many drafts, revisions, and careful editing.

Former 113B, 114B, and 115 students wrote the essays published in this book. They were first-year composition students enrolled in the same class that you now attend; they started where you started. They learned, as you will, to seek help from their peers, professors, supplemental instructors, and the Learning Resource Center in order to achieve the level of writing published in *Wings*.

At the beginning of each essay, to serve as guides to the writing process, we have included critical questions. We have confidence these queries will provoke critical thinking and bring you into the ongoing academic conversation of which these essays are a part. Over the course of your own first-year composition class, you will be assigned similar essays to the ones published in *Wings*. We trust that these essays will act as models of successful first-year writing, and we hope they will inspire, challenge, and motivate you to produce the best writing you can. To discover more fascinating work from your peers, visit the online component to *Wings*: http://newvoices-wings.haydenmcneil.com.

Melisa Malvin-Middleton &
Emily Olson
Wings Editors

Rachel Dulaney &
Jennifer E. Lee
Wings Assistant Editors

Acknowledgments

There are many people who made *Wings* possible, but we would first like to thank our first-year student contributors. This book would not be possible without you. We thank you for having the courage to submit your work; we are honored to have had the opportunity to publish your work. *Wings* belongs to you.

We would also like to express our appreciation to Dr. Irene Clark, who served as an advisor and mentor to the *Wings* staff now and in past years. We would also like to thank Dr. Pamela Bourgeois for her dedication and interest in the work of CSUN's first-year writers. We must convey our deepest thanks to the CSUN English Department staff: Marlene Cooksey, Marjie Seagoe, Frank De La Santo, Tonie Magnum, and Wendy Say. Your hard work, support, and your willingness to always lend a hand, make the English Department a wonderful place.

Wings would not be what it is without the dedicated CSUN composition instructors, Supplemental Instruction leaders, and Learning Resource Center tutors, who invest their time into helping students become the best writers they can be. Thank you to all of those instructors who encourage your students to submit their writing to *Wings*. We are honored to be a part of such a dedicated community of educators. A big thank you to Dr. Jennifer C. Lee and to all those who participated in the *Wings* reading; your help is crucial to the editorial process. Also, a special thanks to the littlest member of our editorial team, Kiera Olson, who was helping us read submissions while in-utero and providing some much needed input as we finalized this issue.

To Barb DeVore and everyone at Hayden-McNeil—thank you for your patience, advisement, and expertise. We are grateful for everything you do to make *Wings* happen.

Finally, we would like to thank Rachel and Jennifer, our assistant editors who put endless amounts of work into the editing process without complaint. This book would not exist without your hard work and dedication.

Preface: A Look Back

"During this semester, I learned how to create a
strong and clear thesis, how to organize my ideas,
the importance of brainstorming, and how to go into
a deeper analysis of different pieces of work."

—Antanay Tarrant

Game, Set, and Match with First-Year Composition

Paulina Silva

Instructor: Terri Silverberg

Critical Question

The author compares the struggle to write a successful essay with the challenges of learning tennis. What comparison would you use to describe your writing process?

Author Statement: *The inspiration behind my cover letter was the fact that I had struggled so much with writing a perfect essay. Everything I wrote never seemed to be good enough. As I sat with writer's block, not having an idea of what to start my cover letter with, I noticed my tennis racket full of spider webs and was reminded of the struggle I faced with tennis. This sparked the idea that both obstacles were related, and although one was a sport and other an academic subject, they were very similar. They were both challenges.*

A couple of years ago, I took private tennis lessons because I wanted to be on the tennis team at my high school. Something about the sport, the serves, strokes, backhands, forehands, overhead smash, lob, and all the footwork, hypnotized me. However, my tennis skills were anything but innate, and that definitely made me regret my decision. Unfortunately, I ended up running nonstop drills and chasing after balls because the only vocabulary that left my coach's mouth was: "YOU'RE YOUNG! IF YOU MISS THE SERVE, YOU PICK UP TENNIS BALLS!" Although tennis seemed to be a simple sport where the goal was to get the ball over the net, I had finally met my match, and it put up an intense fight. Similarly, first year composition was disguised as my love for writing, but in reality was another tennis ball.

First-year composition was my new match. The first play was the essay inspired by the censorship controversy in my reading, "Boston Photographs." In my first essay, "Private Death for All," the citations left me annihilated out on the court and left me with the worst grade I had ever received on any English paper. GAME.

English had always been a strong subject for me, and I was identified as gifted since middle school, so I took pride in my writing. When I saw my grade and my professor's comments, I felt defeated; this was supposed to be an easy "A."

My next game was against the Novak Djokovic of English: MLA citations and using databases to research for my second essay on California's drought, "Not One More Drop." For some reason, while researching through databases, it was difficult to find credible sources that could be used for my topic because I was too accustomed to Google. But just like using my backhand, I had to learn to use the database properly, and once I did, it became easier to find sources to cite. Once again, my returning opponent, citing the sources, took a point but did not defeat me, and I greatly improved. SET.

I revised every essay and appreciated the constructive criticism because like in tennis, practice makes perfect. In my case, it made improvement. I continued to learn from my mistakes. I ran after the balls, annoyed, knowing I could not get worse; I would only improve if I continued to work for it. That's what writing is: patience, practice, and determination. Essay after essay, I improved, and although I have to work on making a more concise and stronger thesis statement in my future writing, I know I will achieve it with practice.

Just like tennis' promotion of persistence, patience, and other skills helped me to succeed in writing, first year composition provides skills that I am able to use in everyday life and in other courses.

I may not be the next Maria Sharapova, but I have gained determination. MATCH.

The Growth of a Writer
Antanay Tarrant

Instructor: Angeline Olliff

Critical Question

In this reflection, the author discusses techniques, such as brainstorming, as ways to overcome the obstacles of starting to write a paper. What prewriting techniques, such as listing, clustering, or freewriting, help you begin writing your papers? Explain.

Author Statement: *For my English portfolio reflection, I really wanted to focus on how I have had major growth as a writer. In my eyes, I have grown from a mediocre writer to an extraordinary writer with the help of this course. I enjoyed this English course, and all of the help I was offered, including the feedback, which really pushed me to be better. This reflection became very important to me while writing it because even though I improved, there is still room for more improvement. The entire semester has been a wonderful experience.*

From middle school all the way through high school, my main goal when it came to writing essays was just to finish the paper and turn it in so that I would never have to look at it again. I never put much thought into my writing for the simple fact that I did not take it seriously. I looked at it as just another assignment given by a teacher that I had to complete by a certain date. Now that I am a first-time freshman in college getting ready to complete my first English course, I can say that this class has helped me become a much better writer than I was before. During this semester, I learned how to create a strong and clear thesis, how to organize my ideas, the importance of brainstorming, and how to go into a deeper analysis of different pieces of work.

The first essay that we were assigned had to deal with rhetorical analysis, and the goal was to analyze two advertisements, then explain how they reflect cultural values in the United States. If I were given this prompt in middle school or high school, I would have stated the obvious: the colors used in these advertisements and what they were trying to sell. However, with the reading we did in class, for example, Hanna Berry's essay "The Fashion Industry: Free to Be an Individual," in which she analyzed every detail in a picture and found the deeper meaning, I was able to read the text and go into in-depth analysis of my advertisements. The more analysis I did, the more I was able to form a thesis for the entire essay, whereas before the analysis, I could not even figure out what my topic would be. Another source that helped me in writing this essay was the article on color psychology that went into detail about what the meaning of almost every color was. With this, I was able to make more sense of why companies choose certain colors and what effect they have on consumers. Without this preparation, I would not have been able to analyze the advertisements as much as I did and come up with a solid thesis.

Along with learning how to analyze different texts, I struggled with the brainstorming process and organizing all of my ideas. For the second essay, the prompt asked us to analyze two completely different articles and use both of them to take a stance on whether or not video game technology is a problem in the United States and to what extent. Heather E. Douglas's article, "The Dark Side of Science," had to do with scientific innovation and how scientists should be held responsible for what people do with their research. On the other hand, in Sam Anderson's essay, "Just One More Game . . . : Angry Birds, Farmville, and Other Hyperaddictive Stupid Games," he expresses how he feels toward the advancement of video games and how in his opinion they are stupid. It became complicated for me to start this essay when I did not know how to use these sources to support my thought that video games are a problem to a certain extent. This issue forced me to brainstorm and get all of my thoughts down on paper, even though it was something I never did. Normally I would jump right into an essay without a second thought, but I could not do it this time. I had to learn how to brainstorm exactly what I wanted to write about so that I could form a clear thesis and make sure my sentences and paragraphs were organized in a way that made sense. At the end of the essay, I noticed that the brainstorming did help me stay organized, and I was able to write about everything that I wanted to.

Now that this class is concluding, I can say with confidence that my writing has improved, and I have grown as a writer. Whether my obstacles were big or small, when it came to my essays, I learned how to overcome them through this class and the different writing strategies that were introduced to us. After this course, I have learned to appreciate the writing process and all of the work it takes to create a well-written essay. While I know that I still have a lot of growing to do as a writer, it is obvious that I have improved over the years. I went from rushing a paper just to complete it on time, to carefully putting together an essay that shows that I tried. I have grown tremendously as a writer just by taking this one course, and I plan to continue to improve how I write over these next few years in college.

THE FIGHT TO THE "A"

Kerriann Pollock

Instructor: Nicole Eschen

CRITICAL QUESTION

How would this portfolio introduction have been different if it had been written in prose? Does the form and genre of the poem add to your understanding of the writer's "fight" to improve her grades? Explain.

Author Statement: *I enjoyed writing this poem because the transition to college level writing was indeed a struggle for me. I believe every freshman that wants an "A" should understand that they will have to work for it.*

The feeling of knowing no one is smarter than your professor;

A love and hate relationship that only grows with time.

No growth is better than the one you experience through your pen.

All the misplaced commas and conjunctions that you can never ignore again.

You learn how to speak better, to hold a better conversation.

Each paper you did not get an "A" on just means a lesson worth taking.

Believing there is an easy way out only leads you down a darker tunnel.

Take the advice, make the paper nice;

There is no such thing as too much editing.

The faster you learn this, the sooner those revisions will become your friend.

Talk to your professors as much as you can.

Utilize your time with them because after a semester, it will come to an end.

The hardest part for me was accepting that all my papers earned a "B."

I always hoped to be a great writer, but now it no longer has to be a dream.

Sharpen your pencils, get your notebook ready, this isn't high school English:

That "A" will not come to you! You have to go get it!

Unveiling the Mythos of America

"Although private prison companies promise to be the immediate relief for states' prison overcrowding problems, due to the nature of government contracts, private prisons have a lucrative incentive to promote mass incarceration."

—Lemuel Dizon

THE AMERICAN MYTH
Francesca Renzulli

Instructor: Anna Dawahare

CRITICAL QUESTION
What is "The American Dream"? According to the author, is the Dream accessible to all people living in America today? Why or why not? Do you agree or disagree with this sentiment? Explain.

Author Statement: *When given the assignment regarding the American Dream, my first thought was that it was going to be tough writing five to seven pages on this subject I have no true care for or opinion toward. So, on my first attempt (the key word here being "first"), I wrote a five and a half page paper on the American Dream, but it was lacking in many departments. I needed to completely start over because, as my professor taught to me in our twenty-minute conversation in the hall after class, the best way to write an essay is to like what you're writing about and assert your voice and opinions via your writing. A subject I do have unending interest and insight into is the world of television. As an aspiring television producer, writer, journalist, or whatever TV-related occupation I land on in the future, I have a better understanding of television than of any other subject. So that's where I started—with a foundation of a subject I enjoy, in relation to the American Dream, and the rest of essay blossomed from there.*

America, known as the land of the free and the home of the brave, is alternately known as the land of opportunity. This opportunity is what many people refer to as "The American Dream." This term was originally coined by the American writer James Truslow Adams in 1931 in his book *The Epic of America*, where he describes this so called dream as a "better and richer" life for everyone, "with opportunity for each according to ability or achievement." This idea has grown into a notion that the United States is a place where you will be accepted no matter where you were born and have the chance to be more successful and prosperous than past generations. However, the Dream is only that, a dream, a fantasy even. But much like the fantastical stories of heroes, princes and princesses, this dream gives people hope. Hope has driven them for decades to not give up on their goals, aspirations, dreams of success, happiness, and prosperity. But the American Dream is a myth. It is advertised through history and different forms of media promising false opportunity. For generations, people have used it as a motivational tool, but the fact of the matter is that the Dream can never become a reality as expectations are too high for most people to achieve, and moreover be pleased with where their lives have landed them.

From an outside perspective, or from one who only looks at the surface, America is a land of freedom, with opportunities galore, equal rights, and strength running through the veins of the country. This is all true, on the surface, but when you pull back the curtain, you would see that the so-called land of liberty is all a façade. This country was founded in hopes of creating a nation with religious freedom and equality by appealing to everyone and discriminating against no one. This was the first lie leaders and motivators told Americans to lure them to the utopian life America can provide. But America could not provide that and still is unable to today. Those who originally arrived here had goals of establishing a country where all men are equal, except the countless slaves they forcibly brought here, of course. This concept of a negative and often ignored element being overshadowed by the promise of equality has occurred time and again throughout history. The negative element being an afterthought is one of the reasons why the American Dream has groomed itself into utter fabrication.

Jack Solomon wrote, "if the American Dream encourages the desire to arrive, to vault about the mass, it also fosters a desire to be popular, to belong" (404). Accordingly, U.S. advertisements fuel Americans' fire for their needs to belong. Beginning with the widely distributed propaganda of the World Wars, and continuing to this day with the constant upgrades of Apple products, Americans want to fit in and will do or buy anything to do so in hopes of reaching the coveted finish line that is the American Dream. Most everybody wants to be popular, for some it's a deep down or subconscious need, and for others, it is right on the surface. Either way, we do things in order to grow in popularity, be it with peers, co-workers, or the entire world. Today, one distinctive way to gain popularity is to be ahead of the trends by having the newest technology in the palm of your hands. Steve Jobs founded Apple with the hopes of making a difference in the technological world, not knowing its unending cultural and media impact in the years to come. He has turned into, even after his death, a ruler, with millions of subjects waiting for him to give them a piece of the American Dream. Jobs seemed to live out his dreams everyday: rich, happy, and doing what he loved. It can be said that one of the reasons Americans rush to stores to buy his products is so they can be like him, even if one's only similarity is a fragile phone. Americans only want to belong, and if they belong to a group with Jobs as one of its members, they will have arrived at the American Dream. But that arrival is an impossible feat.

Handheld technology was not the only catalyst in generating the myth of the Dream. A staple in American culture, television—from reality shows to crime dramas to sitcoms—allows the everyday American to transcend into a different world for thirty minutes or an hour and enjoy someone else's life. While it is great to have the opportunity to rid your mind of your issues for the night, television shows have the ability to coax viewers into believing in the American Dream. Shows like *The Brady Bunch* are prime examples of TV simulating the Dream. *The Brady Bunch* promoted the fantasy that the American Dream is both easily attainable and everlasting. With a family of eight, Mike Brady, the father, has a 9-to-5 job with pay good enough to not only support his happy family but also allow his wife to not have to work and most importantly, afford a maid. This standard of living is something realistically only an upper-class citizen could maintain. The show seamlessly enthralls audiences into believing that they can be like the Bradys someday, so that they can reach the upper class and be as artificially happy as this sitcom family.

The idea that racism is not accounted for when visualizing the American Dream is exhibited in a show like *The Jeffersons*, which gives Americans, specifically African Americans, the false sense of racial equality and equal opportunity in a country primarily run by rich, white individuals. *The Jeffersons* were a happy family; the husband, George Jefferson, much like Mike Brady, provides for his family so much so that finances never seem to be an issue. Additionally, *The Jeffersons* interact with Caucasian neighbors with no sense of difference portrayed on screen. While this is a good value to instill into the young minds of Americans, it gave a false sense of equality in the future for young African Americans. The children of the 1970s and 80s are now today's parents, teachers, and leaders. They grew up watching shows like *The Brady Bunch*, *The Jeffersons*, and later shows in the 90s, such as *Married With Children* and *The Fresh Prince of Bel Air*. These two shows directly contradict the shows of the 70s to early 80s. *Married With Children* and *The Fresh Prince of Bel-Air* aired simultaneously from 1990 to 1997 ("Most Popular"). *Married With Children* followed a dysfunctional, working-class, Caucasian family living in a Chicago suburb. Conversely, *The Fresh Prince of Bel-Air* followed a functional, high-class, African-American family living in Los Angeles' most elite neighborhood, Bel-Air. Both shows create a fantasy world where the American Dream can be attained. While *The Fresh Prince* is more of the widely distributed dream of wealth and safety, *Married With Children* aimed more for the idea that the dream can be having fun, enjoying life, even if you are in the working class of America. These shows, while very different in representing Caucasians and African Americans from *The Brady Bunch* and *The Jeffersons*, both strengthened the mythos of the American Dream. The dream entails that individuals must be happy and content with where their successes have landed them. However, happiness in life is never guaranteed. These sitcoms promote messages that assure American viewers that happiness is a sure thing and everlasting.

We look up to history's greatest leaders and motivators for strength to do what we feel needs to be done to better our lives or the lives of many. Today, however, not only do many Americans look up to these presidents, activists, and pioneers, but they also idolize actors, actresses, and rich reality stars. While the discussion could sprout a plethora of topics on the rich and famous' promotion of materialism and glamour over humble values, one of the most important results of worshipping these idols is that Americans get lost in luxury. They have hopes of reaching their status in the high life; though realistically for many, those luxuries are impossible to obtain. Countless magazines are sold to average American consumers in a place impossible to overlook: the line at the grocery store. The magazines have gaudy headlines of this celebrity buying an Italian villa or another's hundred million dollar divorce settlement. Villas and two hundred million dollar marriages are something that less than one percent of our country has. When lower- and middle-class Americans see these headlines, they are drawn into the myth of success, riches, and luxury; though the truth is that lifestyle is only available to a certain clientele, ones that are not busy gazing at magazines in grocery stores.

While the American Dream promises false opportunity and declares that all Americans have the right to an unguaranteed pursuit of happiness, it does however keep this country afloat. The dream gives people hope. Unlike presidents promising possibilities of hope, change, and equality that most know are never a sure thing, the intangible fantasy of the American Dream can never truly be crushed. The media flaunts the "better and richer" life to its consumers and that cannot be easily stopped. As this nation prospers and develops into an open and honest country so should its products. Advertisements seduce you, technology tempts you, and television entertains you; if the inventors, innovators, and artists of these multimedia outlets can adjust and grow as their country does, disappointment will lessen and fresh starts can be made without the lifelong taunting of the dreamy finish line.

WORKS CITED

"The American Dream." *Library of Congress*. Congress.gov, n.d. Web. 20 Sept. 2014.

"Most Popular TV for 1990-1999." *TV.com*. TV.com, n.d. Web. 20 Sept. 2014.

Solomon, Jack. "Masters of Desire: The Culture of American Advertising." Putnam Publishing Group, 1989. *North Carolina University*. Web. 20 Sept. 2014.

No Imprisonment for Nonviolent Crimes
Sarah Bustillo

Instructor: Terri Silverberg

Critical Question

The author effectively weaves in outside sources to support her argument against wasteful imprisonment for nonviolent crimes. Would the essay have been as effective without the use of outside support? Why or why not?

Author Statement: *I had a very fun and rewarding time writing "No Imprisonment for Nonviolent Crimes." I enjoyed the research process the most because I truly do value learning new information. When researching for this essay, I learned many things about the American government and prison system and what poor conditions overpopulated prisons are keeping their inmates in. Writing this essay allowed me to form my own opinions about certain government regulations and policies that I truly had no strong opinion about. I am thankful for the information I have learned and the opinions I have formed from writing this essay.*

According to William Spelman, a professor at the LBJ School of Public Affairs at the University of Texas, Austin, the United States has the highest documented incarceration rate in the world, making up a quarter of the entire world population. With a population of 2.4 million prison inmates, the U.S. spends around $6.3 billion per year on prisons (Spelman 30). After decades of arresting all sorts of criminals, the country is now faced with an enormous prison population. There are conflicting views on the proper methods to resolve this issue. Some believe that people charged with nonviolent crimes should not be sent to prison. Others feel that being selective about who is sent to prison will have negative repercussions. Although people should be punished for disobeying the law, in order to reduce prison overcrowding and spending, the government should not imprison those who commit nonviolent crimes.

The "tough on crime" movement refers to a set of policies that make punishment a primary response to crime. The 1980s and 1990s brought the enactment of numerous legislative measures including mandatory minimum sentences, "truth-in-sentencing" laws that restrict or abolish parole and early release, and many other proposals that create longer and harsher penalties. These policies and the country's focus on reducing crime have led to an enormous increase in drug arrests, overpopulated prisons, and overspending (Spelman 35-36). Because of this, America needs to abandon the "tough on crime" rhetoric to reduce the prison population and spending.

One of the main causes of prison overcrowding is the incarceration of nonviolent drug offenders. Lahny R. Silva, a Juris Doctor from the University of Connecticut, says that in federal prisons in 2010, fifty-three percent of the prisoners were convicted for drug offenses, while robbery made up four percent, and homicide made up one percent (158-59). This means that more than half of the prison population in America consists of nonviolent drug offenders. According to the report, "Public Safety, Public Spending: Forecasting America's Prison Population 2007-2011," if the government was to stop imprisoning people for nonviolent crimes, the overpopulation of state and federal prisons would immediately begin to decrease, and the country's spending and prison violence rate would go down (240). By incarcerating nonviolent criminals, the country is wasting the space that could have been used to imprison violent criminals.

Another reason the government should avoid incarcerating nonviolent criminals is the country could spend less money on prisons. The *Federal Sentencing Reporter* discusses how every dollar spent on prisons is a dollar not spent preparing for the next Hurricane Katrina, educating young people, providing health care to the elderly, or repairing roads and bridges ("Public" 251). The United States has been burying itself in debt for years, and the spending for prisons is only making this debt worse ("Public" 236). To keep prisoners guarded, housed, fed, and clothed, the United States spends an average annual cost of $22,000 per inmate, with $33,000 for maximum security (Silva 163). This amount of spending is a social threat; because, as it continues, it will create a weak economy and a larger underclass (Spelman 42). Rather than spending thousands of dollars on prisons, America should incarcerate less nonviolent criminals and save that money to fund education, healthcare, and city repairs.

Prison overpopulation has resulted in a lack of resources and space. For example, according to Donald Specter, the director of the Prison Law Office in Berkeley, California, some California prisons have so little space for inmates to sleep that they have triple-bunked gymnasiums, which have reached 300 percent of their intended capacity (194). By refraining from sending nonviolent offenders to prison, more resources and room will be available for the dangerous and violent offenders, such as: murderers, rapists, and sexual and aggravated assault assailants. In California, as well as in many other states, overcrowding often results in violence and sometimes deadly harm to prisoners and prison staff (Specter 194). The public can even be harmed physically and financially because of prison violence. For example, in 2009, a riot that broke out in a prison near Los Angeles resulted in millions of dollars in damage and hundreds of injured prisoners. This kind of violence is common in prisons because inmates are more confined since many programs and recreational spaces have been eliminated (Specter 195). If the country or the state wishes to resolve prison violence and lack of resources, then it must first lower the number of people incarcerated for nonviolent crimes.

Prisons in the West, the Midwest, and the South have the fastest growing inmate population according to Joseph L. Martin, Deputy Sheriff at the Tuscaloosa County Sheriff's Office in Alabama; Bronwen Lichtenstein, an Associate Professor and Director of Graduate Studies in the Department of Criminal Justice at the University of Alabama; Robert B. Jenkot, an Assistant Professor in the Department of Sociology at Coastal Carolina University; and David R. Forde, Associate Dean and Professor of Sociology at the University of North Texas, Dallas. Although southern prisons are among the most crowded in the United States, they are still underfunded and understaffed (Martin et al. 88). This lack of funding and staff can greatly affect the well-being of inmates and prison workers.

In Alabama, where the inmate to officer ratio is the highest in America, a study conducted by the Alabama Department of Corrections showed that working in overcrowded and understaffed prisons can significantly affect a worker's health. Out of sixty-six participants, forty-three staff members felt they had difficulty in monitoring inmates and short tempers from an excessive workload because of prison overcrowding. Out of the same sixty-six participants, thirty-seven had high levels of stress; nine had a high risk of infectious disease; and six had a risk of hypertension and cardiovascular disease. Still, some think these health effects are excuses by prison staff for their poor management and lack of officer training (Martin et al. 100). However, these statistics show the physical and emotional effects of high incarceration rates and overcrowding on prison staff.

Supporters of harsher punishment stress that many criminal acts are connected to drug addiction. Their belief is when people are selling, carrying, or under the influence of drugs, the possibility of them committing crimes increases. These people also believe that minor crimes often lead to major crimes, and imprisoning nonviolent offenders for minor crimes will prevent them from committing major ones. Attorney General Michael Mukasey, for instance, has fought to keep people convicted of drug offenses in prison with little to no opportunity for early release, saying that many of them are among the most serious and violent offenders (qtd. in Silva 172-73). However, there is no evidence to support his statement.

Although spending less money on fewer prisoners seems to be the most obvious solution to overspending, supporters of "tough on crime" policies believe otherwise. Supporters often state that the imprisonment of a criminal can prevent between two and seven crimes, which saves potential victims between $4,000 and $19,000 per year. However, as Spelman points out, "if each [inmate] reduces costs by no more than $19,000 but costs us $20,000 to $40,000 [to care for], then do we need this many [inmates]?" (30). Kent Scheidegger and Michael Rushford, the Legal Director and President of the Criminal Justice Legal Foundation, say that, "the simple truth is that imprisonment works. . . . Locking up criminals for longer periods reduces the level of crime. The benefits of doing so far offset the costs" (64). They believe this because putting violent and nonviolent criminals in prison reduces the number of future victims, thereby reducing the costs that the victim and society would have had to pay. However, there is no basis for claiming that a prisoner who stays in prison for an additional year will commit fewer crimes when they're released.

Many people argue that longer mandatory minimum sentences should be given to all people who break the law to ensure uniformity in sentencing criminals. Also, they believe that potential criminals and repeat offenders are more likely to avoid committing crimes because they are aware of their sentences if they are convicted (Silva 198). Mandatory minimum sentences also reflect "a societal judgment that certain offenses demand a specified minimum sanction and thereby ensure that anyone who commits such a crime cannot avoid a just punishment . . . [it also] ensures that a sentence is fairly given to the crime, not the person" (Spelman 52). However, while fairness is important, there are nevertheless many nonviolent criminals who receive sentences that are disproportionate to their crimes.

Aside from the costs to society, there are costs the prisoner has to pay. The claim that mandatory minimum sentences for offenders of minor, nonviolent crimes are fair is hypocritical because they often receive an unfair amount of time in prison for their crimes. Phyllis Goldfarb, a professor of Clinical Law at the Jacob Burns Foundation, describes an example of unfair sentences for nonviolent drug crimes. Dorothy Gaines, a former nurse and mother of three, was sentenced in Alabama to nineteen years and seven months in prison for her role in a crack-cocaine conspiracy. At the time, Gaines was unaware that her boyfriend was secretly selling drugs. Although police could find no evidence of Gaines' involvement, she was found guilty based solely on her co-defendant's testimony (Goldfarb 280). Gaines should not have received the punishment that she did, but because of mandatory minimum sentences, she was forced to spend years of her life in prison.

In another case, in 2007, Telisha Watkins, a financially desperate single mother of four with no criminal history, received a twenty-year prison sentence in North Carolina for arranging a cocaine deal for an old neighbor who was actually a police informant. Watkins thought that the deal she was arranging only involved cocaine, but there was also crack in the package. Her estimated release date is 2024, while the dealer, who actually sold the drugs, was released in March of 2008 (Specter 198). How is it considered fair for Watkins to receive a sentence that is sixteen years longer than that of the actual drug dealer? If fairness is the goal, then mandatory minimums should not be used when sentencing a nonviolent offender.

"Tough on crime" policies that give criminals longer and harsher punishments aren't just frustrating many Americans; many other countries have started to develop an unfavorable opinion as well. Scheideggar and Rushford explain that criminologists in other countries "are appalled by the number and length of U.S. prison sentences. The enormous figures have drawn contempt from European critics, saying that the United States has been following its pursuit on the war on crime with an ignorant fanaticism" (62). Freidrich Losel, Director of the Institute of Criminology at the University of Cambridge, says that countries such as Australia, Canada, and England have higher rates of nonviolent crime than the United States, but they still have a lower incarceration rate (517). The fact that those countries have an equal or lower overall crime rate than the United States shows how extreme and unnecessary America's "war on crime" is.

Around the world, people who commit nonviolent crimes are less likely to receive prison time than those in the United States, which incarcerates for the smallest crime, such as passing a bad check (Losel 517). Ryan King, a policy analyst for *The Sentencing Project*, mentions that many European countries feel the amount of prison time some criminals are forced to serve in the United States is inhumane (50). Burglars in the United States get an average of sixteen months in prison, compared to the five months given in Canada and the seven months in England. Keep in mind that crime rate in Canada has been closely parallel to America's for nearly forty years, but the imprisonment rate has remained stable. Therefore, even with the United States paying billions of dollars to arrest and imprison as many criminals as possible, the crime rate is still relatively the same as a country that does not pursue and imprison criminals as obsessively. America's harsh punishments are created with good intentions, but those intentions alone do not make good policy; results are also necessary.

Instead of imprisoning criminals for every crime, America should approve of reforms similar to those presented in the state of California, such as the Holder prison reform package and Proposition 47. On Tuesday June 10, 2014, Attorney General Eric H. Holder, Jr. offered his full support of the new Justice Department policy. *The Buffalo News* stated that if the prison policy is passed, low-level, nonviolent drug offenders with no ties to gangs or large-scale drug organizations won't be charged with long, mandatory sentence offenses ("Sentencing" A6). Similarly, Proposition 47 in California states that those who commit certain low-level offenses such as: check fraud, drug possession, forgery, and shoplifting, will receive lighter sentences as long as they had no serious or violent crimes on their record. *The San Jose Mercury News* stated that Proposition 47 could impact nearly 40,000 people and save money in the low hundreds of millions annually. Both policies would reduce prison overcrowding in California because fewer individuals would be sent to prison for nonviolent crimes, and people who are already in prison for those offenses can be resentenced, sent to county jails, released, receive supervised probation, or receive court-ordered drug treatment, all of which cost the state less money ("Public" A14). A June field poll found that fifty-seven percent of Californians support the initiative, with nineteen percent undecided ("Public" A14). This support for Proposition 47 demonstrates how state residents are increasingly frustrated with spending on prisons.

By being more selective about who is sent to prison, the United States can lower its enormous prison population and spending. Not only is it immoral to keep hundreds or thousands of people in prisons with limited space, but it is also a significant misuse of America's money. With crime rates in the U.S. similar to those of countries that incarcerate less, one can see the waste that the "tough on crime" movement has caused. By not imprisoning people who commit nonviolent crimes, eliminating harsh mandatory minimum sentences, and making use of community and rehabilitation programs, America can save time and money.

WORKS CITED

Goldfarb, Phyllis. "Counting the Drug War's Female Casualties." *The Journal of Gender, Race & Justice* 6 (2002): 277-473. Web. 07 Dec. 2014.

King, Ryan S. "A Change of Course: Developments in State Sentencing Policy and Their Implications for the Federal System." *Federal Sentencing Reporter* 22.1 (2009): 48-52. Web. 07 Dec. 2014.

Losel, Friedrich. "Counterblast: The Prison Overcrowding Crisis." *The Howard Journal of Criminal Justice* 46.5 (2007): 512-19. Web. 07 Dec. 2014.

Martin, Joseph, Bronwen Lichtenstein, Robert Jenkot, and David Forde. "Correctional Officers' Responses to Prison Crowding." *The Prison Journal* 92.1 (2012): 88-105. Web. 07 Dec. 2014.

"Public Safety, Public Spending: Forecasting America's Prison Population 2007-2011." *Federal Sentencing Reporter* 19.4 (2007): 234-52. Web. 07 Dec. 2014.

"Public Safety Will Improve with Prop. 47." *San Jose Mercury News.* 26 Sept. 2014: A14. Web. 07 Dec. 2014.

Scheidegger, Kent, and Michael Rushford. "The Social Benefits of Confining Habitual Criminals." *Stanford Law & Policy Review* 11 (2000): 59-64. Web. 07 Dec. 2014.

"Sentencing Disgrace: Policy Setting Mandatory Minimums Takes the Justice out of the Legal System." *Buffalo News* 10 Dec. 2013: A6. Web. 07 Dec. 2014.

Silva, Lahny R. "Clean Slate: Expanding Expungements and Pardons for Non-Violent Federal Offenders." *University of Cincinnati Law Review* 79.1 (2010): 155-205. Web. 07 Dec. 2014.

Specter, Donald. "Everything Revolves Around Overcrowding: The State of California's Prisons." *Federal Sentencing Reporter* 22.3 (2010): 194-99. Web. 07 Dec. 2014.

Spelman, William. "Crime, Cash, and Limited Options: Explaining the Prison Boom." *Criminology & Public Policy* 8.1 (2009): 29-77. Web. 07 Dec. 2014.

SHOULD SOLITARY CONFINEMENT BE ABOLISHED FROM THE U.S. PRISON SYSTEM?

Caroline Marriott

Instructor: Erin Delaney

CRITICAL QUESTION

This author addresses a counterargument to strengthen her position that U.S. prisons should limit the use of solitary confinement. Can you locate the counterargument within the essay? To what extent does the author's consideration of opposing views help promote her stance? Explain.

Author Statement: *My inspiration behind writing this essay this is the experience I had volunteering at HMP Stocken, England in the visiting room and children's play area. After speaking to the prisoners' relatives, I realized how much inmates are affected by isolation, especially experiencing mental health problems. Having gained an insight into the U.K. prison system, I thought that it would be interesting to explore the U.S. prison system and research solitary confinement.*

Solitary confinement is "the practice of imprisoning people in solitary cells, without access to any human contact or stimulation, as a method of rehabilitation" (Center for Constitutional Rights). Despite only having 5% of the world's population, the U.S. has 25% of the world's prisoners. The 2000 U.S. Census states that there are "over 81,000 inmates in some form of solitary isolation in the U.S.—roughly the total number of all prisoners in the whole of the U.K." (Dimon). A large controversy surrounds the incorporation of solitary confinement into U.S. prisons. It is justified as essential in protecting inmates and prison staff from violent assault. However, the repressive conditions of solitary confinement have negative consequences on the mental health of inmates, so the practice should be abolished.

The physical conditions of solitary confinement have changed over the years. In the nineteenth century, solitary consisted of "dark and dirty underground holes," whereas in the twenty-first century, solitary consists of "well-lit, sterile boxes" (CCR). Although the appearance of the cells is somewhat improved, prisoners are still "detained inside cramped, concrete, windowless [eight-by-ten foot] cells in a state of near-total solitude between 22 and 24 hours a day" (CCR). When inmates are allowed out of their cells, they remain in handcuffs and shackles and are only allowed to pace up and down alone. The cells are very restrictive and are furnished with only a basic toilet, shower, and bed. The only way that an inmate can communicate from inside the cell is through a locked port in the door; the slot is only large enough for passing a food tray. There are very limited communication allowances; inmates are often deprived of contact visits and telephone calls, and mail is censored. There is no privacy; inmates are under constant video surveillance.

Out of the aforementioned 81,000 inmates, 25,000 of these are assigned to supermax prisons. Consisting of solid doors and being practically soundproofed, supermax prisons are intended to foster maximum segregation. Pelican Bay State Prison, a Special Housing Unit (SHU) in California, which opened on December 1, 1989, is described by the CCR as, the "most restrictive prison in California and one of the harshest 'supermaximum' prisons in the country." More than "500 of Pelican Bay's [SHU] prisoners have been held in solitary for over 10 years" and are confined to only a six-by-eight foot cell; it is not surprising that inmates develop mental health problems (McCarthy). The most common reason for prisoners to be assigned to the SHU is for gang affiliation. Inmates are often labeled gang members if they are seen waving to an already confirmed member or if they display specific tattoos that are affiliated with the gang. The only way out of the SHU is to "debrief" or to offer incriminating information, such as the "gang status of other prisoners" (Clark). Review of the need for SHU happens only every six years; it should occur every three years so that the prison officials consider current and relevant information.

Solitary confinement has both positive and negative consequences on mental health. When determining whether or not solitary should be abolished, four factors must be addressed. Karen Harrison, University of Hull, Lecturer of Law, highlights these factors as 1) individual: inmate background and previous health issues; 2) environmental: physical conditions of solitary confinement and provisions for inmates; 3) the reason for and duration of confinement: punishment or own protection; and 4) routine: time outside the cell and degree of human interaction. For example, some prisons introduced remote controls to open the cell gates replacing the guard, who was possibly the only person that the inmate interacted with.

On one hand, it could be argued that solitary confinement has numerous positive aspects, so it should not be abolished. Solitary benefits the individual inmates by providing them with time to reflect on their criminal behavior, acknowledge their mistakes, and develop a clearer view of life. Without solitary, prisoners may never learn from their crimes. Inmates will hopefully learn what is morally right and wrong, which will likely reduce the chance of them reoffending. Once released back into society, they may wish to even volunteer their services to those they hurt; for example, a thief may work with the police to provide inside knowledge of the techniques that criminals use to burgle homes. Solitary can improve inmate behavior; for example, inmates with rebellious tendencies may become more docile because they realize that violence and crime is not always the solution. Also, solitary benefits society because it removes dangerous people from the streets, creating a safer community, especially for children. By isolating violent criminals from other inmates and staff, the levels of prison harassment decrease. Moreover, solitary acts as a deterrent to future crimes, which the general prison population may not do. If dangerous criminals are not punished and isolated, society would feel it unjust.

On the other hand, the negative consequences outweigh the positives, so solitary confinement should be abolished. Firstly, according to Elizabeth Landau, it has profound physical impact on the brain. Autopsies of inmates with severe depression have shown that "the orchestration of brain and activity of genes in their brains is messed up" (Landau). Huda Akil, a neuroscientist at the University of Michigan, reported that stress and chronic depression are "associated with a shrinking of the hippocampus, a sea-horse shaped brain area critical for memory, spatial recognition and controlling one's emotions" and that "the longer the depression is untreated, the more the hippocampus shrinks" (qtd. in Landau). This evidence reinforces the detrimental effects of solitary on prisoner mental health, such as some prisoners experiencing a vegetative state. The greater the sentence in solitary, the more damage done to the brain.

Secondly, inmates in solitary confinement, especially those in supermax prisons, experience many psychological problems; 45 percent of supermax residents have serious mental illnesses. Peter Scharff Smith states, according to one federal judge, putting mentally-ill prisoners in isolated confinement "is the mental equivalent of putting an asthmatic in a place with little air." Considering that society does not support the practice of restricting an asthmatic's access to air, society should not support the practice of isolating a prisoner from human interaction. With this said, it is very concerning that supermax prisons have "more than three times as many men and women with mental illnesses as are held in mental health hospitals in the U.S." (National Alliance on Mental Illness). The conditions of solitary are so severe that 8–19% of U.S. prisoners have psychiatric disorders "that result in significant functional disabilities" (Landau). Common psychological mental health problems include: anger, such as uncontrollable rage; anxiety, such as feeling that the walls are coming in on them; depression; insomnia; paranoia and psychosis; cognitive disturbances, such as distortion of time; and perceptual distortions, ranging from hypersensitivity (to noise and smells) to hallucinations, such as hearing voices when no-one is talking and seeing people in the cell when no-one is there. For some, the line between reality and fantasy becomes blurred; for example, it is very common for inmates to create imaginary friends. The brain may be attempting to generate its own stimulation in response to the lack of outside stimuli.

Thirdly, solitary confinement should be abolished because of the increased incidents of deliberate self-harm and suicide in prisons. Suicide rates are higher in isolated units, compared to those of general prison populations. Amnesty International reported that in September 2013, a prisoner, who had been held in solitary confinement at ADX (Administrative Maximum facility near Florence, Colorado) for more than a decade, had developed a severe mental illness and hung himself in his cell. Isolation is so distressing that prisoners forget what it feels like to be human. Inmates have testified that self-mutilation acts as a means of liberation from intolerable frustration and pain; it is extremely unhealthy that prisoners view cutting as a way to remind themselves that they are alive. Former prisoners said: "[I was] rocking myself back and forth and banging my head against the wall. In the absence of sensation, it's hard to convince yourself that you're really there. . . . I started smashing up the cell. I refused to eat [and drink]. I was totally paranoid. I started sipping my own urine because I thought they were trying to poison me. I resorted to self-injury" (Shalev).

Before it is abolished, the conditions of solitary confinement must be reviewed because, as Piper Kerman illustrates in *Orange Is The New Black*, there are limited resources to treat mentally ill prisoners. According to Jeffrey L. Metzner, M.D., "mental health services in segregation units are typically limited to psychotropic medication, a healthcare clinician stopping at the cell front to ask how the prisoner is doing (i.e., mental health rounds), and occasional meetings in private with a clinician." Metzner explains, "individual therapy; group therapy; structured educational, recreational, or life-skill-enhancing activities . . . are usually not available because of insufficient resources and rules requiring prisoners to remain in their cells." The lack of treatment options available is a major problem; if inmates do not receive sufficient mental health care, they may develop SHU Syndrome, a mental condition combining all of the aforementioned psychological symptoms but all to the extreme scale.

Moreover, it could be argued that solitary confinement is counterproductive. If prisoners are "not mentally ill when entering an isolation unit, by the time they are released, their mental health has been severely compromised" (American Friends Service Committee). This report conveys that solitary actually worsens prisoners' mental states and potentially causes irreversible damage. Dr. Janis Petzel, the president of Maine's People's Alliance says, "Solitary creates and exacerbates mental illness and cripples social skills. Prisoners who have experienced segregation and who are released back into the community re-lapse back into criminal behavior sooner and more aggressively than their general prison population counterparts" (qtd. in Chin). Researchers at the University of Washington strongly supported this statement by releasing a report in 2007 showing that 69% of pris-oners released from solitary confinement back into society reoffend; whereas, only 44% of prisoners from general prison populations reoffend. The goal of solitary confinement is to protect the public and ensure their safety, but instead, it damages community well-being and is a failure. Kirsten Weir, of the American Psychological Association, highlights that inmates find it difficult to transition back into society after experiencing solitary, as they are not prepared; prisoners who have been locked away in segregation for so long become fearful of their own thoughts and actions. In turn, when released back into society, for-mer criminals may either voluntarily shut themselves away in isolation because they can't remember how to interact with others, and therefore, do not live normal lives, or they may continue to harm other people, such as plotting to murder the person who put them in prison because they have had so much time alone to think and plan new crimes (they have nothing else to do). Either way, there are very limited positive outcomes. Another reason for the abolishment of solitary is that it is very expensive: "It costs about $78,000 a year to house someone in the federal prison system in solitary. . . . That's three times as much as it costs to put somebody in a regular prison unit" (Johnson). The money spent on segregation could be invested in more worthwhile projects, such as financially assisting charities. Providing money to a children's cancer charity would be more beneficial to the community as a whole, as family members would be treated and saved from an illness, rather than money being spent on isolating human beings and, in turn, creating illnesses.

Furthermore, international human rights activists argue that solitary confinement is un-just and should be completely abolished. In August 2011, Juan Mendez, at the United Nations, stated, "even 15 days in solitary confinement constitutes torture or cruel, inhu-mane or degrading treatment or punishment, and 15 days is the limit after which irre-versible harmful psychological effects can occur" (CCR). However, many prisoners in the U.S. are held in isolation for much longer than this. The U.S. was established on the prin-ciple of liberty, but the government is depriving their citizens of this basic human right.

A possible solution may be to reduce the duration that prisoners are assigned to segregation and "transfer . . . [them to a] general prison population for several months before being released" (Weir). A study of the solitary inmates at the Western Prison in Copenhagen showed a decline in mental health symptoms soon after inmates had been transferred. This indicates that mental health problems in prisons could be avoided by abolishing solitary confinement. The University of Washington stated that in 2007, the "recidivism rate dropped by 46 percent" when prisoners were released from general prison populations (Walters).

Solitary confinement has more negative than positive consequences. The conditions and duration of segregation are too harsh, often causing irreversible mental damage. Solitary is not only harmful to the inmates, but also to the community as a whole, as prisoners often become more violent. Long-term solitary confinement should be abolished because it "has no restorative or rehabilitative purpose. It is not a sustainable solution to legitimate security concerns" (Clark). However, if the practice were to remain active, it should only be used in exceptional circumstances and only for short periods of time. The duration in solitary confinement should be reduced by transferring prisoners to general prison populations sooner. The review of solitary confinement should occur more regularly.

Works Cited

American Friends Service Committee. "What Is Solitary Confinement?" *American Friends Service Committee.* American Friends Service Committee, n.d. Web. 28 Nov. 2014.

Amnesty International. "USA: Prisoners Held in Extreme Solitary Confinement in Breach of International Law." *Amnesty International.* Amnesty International, 16 July 2014. Web. 28 Nov. 2014.

Center for Constitutional Rights. "Torture: The Use of Solitary Confinement in U.S. Prisons." *Center for Constitutional Rights.* Center for Constitutional Rights, n.d. Web. 29 Nov. 2014.

Chin, Ben. "Solitary Confinement is Counterproductive." *Sun Journal.* 21 Mar. 2010. *ProQuest.* Web. 29 Nov. 2015.

Clark, Monica. "California Prisoners Suspend Hunger Strike Against Solitary Confinement." *National Catholic Reporter.* National Catholic Reporter, 13 Sept. 2013. Web. 29 Nov. 2014.

Dimon, Laura. "80,000 Americans Suffer From a Cruel and Unusual Practice Most Countries Abolished." *MIC.* MIC, 12 Mar. 2014. Web. 25 Nov. 2014.

Harrison, Karen. "Death Row Phenomenon, Death Row Syndrome and Their Effect On Capital Cases in The U.S." 2010. *Internet Journal of Criminology.* Web. 25 Nov. 2014.

Johnson, Carrie. "Solitary Confinement Costs $78K Per Inmate and Should be Curbed, Critics Say." *North County Public Radio.* North Country Public Radio, 25 Feb. 2014. Web. 29 Nov. 2014.

Kerman, Piper. *Orange Is the New Black: My Year in a Women's Prison.* New York: Spiegel & Grau, 2011. Print.

Landau, Elizabeth. "Solitary Confinement: 29 Years in A Box." *CNN Health.* CNN, 23 Feb. 2014. Web. 25 Nov. 2014.

McCarthy, Kevin. "Pelican Bay: Solitary Confinement Is Pure Torture." *San Jose Mercury News.* San Jose Mercury News, 25 Sept. 2013. Web. 25 Nov. 2014.

Metzner, Jeffery. L. "Solitary Confinement and Mental Illness in U.S. Prisons: A Challenge for Medical Ethics." *Human Rights Watch. The Journal of the American Academy of Psychiatry and the Law,* 01 Mar. 2010. Web. 25 Nov. 2014.

National Alliance on Mental Illness. "Solitary Confinement Fact Sheet." *National Alliance on Mental Illness.* NAMI, n.d. Web. 29 Nov. 2014.

Smith, Peter. S. "The Effects of Solitary Confinement on Prison Inmates: A Brief History and Review of the Literature." *Crime and Justice.* 34.1 (2006): 441-528. *The University of Chicago Press.* Web. 25 Nov. 2014.

Shalev, Sharon. "The Health Effects of Solitary Confinement." *Solitary Confinement.* Solitary Confinement, 2014. Web. 29 Nov. 2014.

Walters, Joanna. "Solitary Confinement: Inside America's Dreaded Isolation Cells." *Telegraph.* Telegraph, 16 Jul. 204. Web. 29 Nov. 2014.

Weir, Kirsten. "Alone, In 'The Hole.'" *American Psychological Association.* American Psychological Association, May 2012. Web. 25 Nov. 2014.

PROFITS OVER RESPONSIBILITY

Lemuel Dizon

Instructor: Erin Delaney

CRITICAL QUESTION

This essay makes a strong logical appeal to persuade its audience. To what degree is this an effective way to convince an audience, and how does the author go beyond merely informing them of the problems addressed in the essay? Explain.

Author Statement: *My main purpose in writing this essay is not to persuade but rather to inform people of an issue that I believe to be relevant. I choose this specific argument because it represents a larger theme affecting our government today. It is not privatization but rather how government could be so easily influenced by the needs of the few, not just by money but because of the negligence of the masses. It is my belief that the more informed the people are about politics, the more equal and fair a nation could be.*

Over the past four decades, the U.S. experienced a spike in growth of the prison population. In fact, the prison population boom has reached the point where, according to the American Civil Liberties Union (ACLU), "the United States incarcerates approximately 2.3 million people" (11). The ACLU also found that the U.S. has 25% of the world's prisoners (11). To put it into perspective, the U.S. only has 5% of the world's population. The fact that the U.S. has 25% of the world's prisoners, means that out of every country, the U.S. has to deal with the most detainees. Dealing with the largest proportion of prisoners to population comes with a substantial burden. As the inmate population continued to balloon, states across the nation had to deal with financial and labor burdens of prison overcrowding that became worse as time passed. During 1984, the first private prison company Corrections Corporations of America (CCA) emerged, as they were contracted a Tennessee facility to manage. Contracting with private prisons became a popular choice for states as private prisons promised to alleviate states' bloated state budgets due to mass incarceration. Despite the fact that private prisons offer immediate relief, these corporations have an incentive to increase or at least sustain prison overcrowding, showing that private prisons are not the solution to overcrowding.

Although private prison companies promise to be the immediate relief for states' prison overcrowding problems, due to the nature of government contracts, private prisons have a lucrative incentive to promote mass incarceration. These incentives to sustain or increase overcrowding exist because private prisons earn revenue for each prisoner that they house. Consequently to ensure profits for their investors, private prisons have sought to increase the number of prisoners they house because more prisoners means more money. There are three ways private prisons could increase the number of prisoners they have. An easy way to illustrate it is to compare it to hotels. Hotels market to get more people to fill their rooms, just as private prisons' lobby for contracts to get more prisoners into their cells. This is how hotels and private prisons ensure maximum profit.

To expand their capacity, both private prisons and hotels obtain more facilities. To create loyal customers, hotels aim to give a great experience to customers in the hopes that they would return, while private prisons aim to give a terrible rehabilitation experience in the hopes that inmates would re-commit a crime and return. In the end, private prisons do help alleviate the pressures of overcrowding from states, but instead of stopping mass incarceration, they help promote it.

Expanding on the idea of how private prisons sought to create loyal customers, high recidivism must be explained. In the context of prisons, recidivism pertains to former inmates that re-commit a crime and return to prison. High recidivism means more jail time, and more jail time means more money. In fact, in 2008, according to an independent study of Oklahoma prisons, "private prison inmate groups had a greater hazard of recidivism than did public inmate groups" (qtd. in ACLU 30). Regardless of the fact that many private prison companies claim to have a sound rehabilitation program, according to Mark Cowling, a journalist for *Prison Legal News*, private prisons do not "measure recidivism, or the rate at which their inmates reoffend after they're released." Which means that they do not have a factual basis to make their claims. In reality, there is no real incentive for good rehabilitation programs as it will cost more and lower recidivism rates.

The contracts that private prisons use to obtain more prisoners are low-crime taxes and occupancy guarantee clauses. Typically, if a state wants a private prison to build or take over a facility so that the state may alleviate its overcrowding issues, that state must sign a contract with the private prison. Moreover, based on a report by In the Public Interest (ITPI), a resource center on privatization and responsible contracting, "65 percent of the private prison contracts . . . included occupancy guarantees in the form of quotas or required payments for empty prison cells (a "low-crime tax")" (2). In short, states that seek help from private prisons must either guarantee those prisons will be filled or tax citizens a fee (essentially a "low-crime tax") whenever there are empty beds. Contracts are essentially Priceline for private prisons. Priceline helps hotels stay full, just as contracts help private prisons stay full. However, unlike Priceline, contracts encourage state politicians to send more people to prison rather than taxing their constituents, as it would hurt them in their future campaigns. As a result, pro-incarceration laws are made, laws that send more people to jail.

The last and most effective method that the private prison industry uses in order to increase incarceration is the promotion of pro-incarceration laws through lobbying. Coupled with contracts that states have to sign, the private prison companies have been successful in the creation of pro-incarceration laws. Although private prison companies deny lobbying for pro-incarceration laws, in an SEC (U.S. Security and Exchange Commission) report, a 2010 file from the CCA conceded that: "The demand for our facilities and services could be adversely affected by the relaxation of enforcement efforts, leniency in conviction or parole standards and sentencing practices or through the decriminalization of certain activities that are currently proscribed by our criminal laws" (19). This shows that in order to secure their profits, they must influence legislation and create pro-incarceration laws or at least maintain laws that contribute to mass incarceration. In addition, with the same 2010 Annual Report, the CCA states, "We believe we have been successful in increasing the number of residents in our care and continue to pursue a number of initiatives intended to further increase our occupancy and revenue," clearly showing their intent to influence legislation (16).

To effectively lobby politicians to create legislation that appeals to their needs, private prison companies spend millions of dollars. According to Truthloader, "between 2002 and 2012 the CCA, along with Geo Group Inc. and Management and Training Corporation (MTC) spent around $45 million dollars on lobbying state and federal government," and that's not all, "these three companies also pour hundreds and thousands of dollars every year into the election campaigns of governors, state legislators and judges." By the profiteering nature of private prisons, when these industries spend large sums to lobby, it is obvious that they expect a lucrative outcome. In fact, to increase their influence over legislation they partnered with The American Legislative Exchange Council (ALEC). ALEC is a conservative organization, "comprised of state legislators, business professionals, and private corporations and seeks to build partnerships between state legislators and the private business sector," as noted in a publication by Ashton and Petteruti, where they have also found that: Since the 1980s and 1990s, ALEC facilitated the production of model bills focusing on mandatory minimums, three strikes laws (giving 25 years to life in prison for repeat offenses), and, truth-in-sentencing legislation (requiring people to serve most or all of their time without chance for parole)" (28-29). ALEC's tough-on-crime approach meshes well with the private prison business model, as tougher laws have a large contribution to mass incarceration, which translates to profits for the private prison industry. Unfortunately for private prisons, according to the Federal Bureau of Investigation, crimes have been slowly declining in the past decade. With beds needing to be filled, private prison companies have become more aggressive, actively attempting to increase incarceration rates.

With the newfound union with ALEC, the private prison industry has looked for new potential criminals to jail, which are undocumented immigrants. With anti-immigration laws, undocumented immigrants are criminalized, guaranteeing private prisons a constant stream of prisoners to lock up for profit. This anti-immigration law was Arizona's *The Support Our Law Enforcement and Safe Neighborhoods Act* (SB 1070). Essentially, this law allows police officers to stop people for looking Hispanic and detaining them if they weren't carrying citizenship papers or green cards. According to a case study by Ashton and Petteruti:

> [SB 1070] was originally conceived and drafted at an ALEC meeting that included officials from CCA. When the legislation was brought to the Arizona statehouse floor as a bill in January 2010, 36 legislators co-sponsored it—two-thirds of whom either attended the meeting where the bill was written or were members of ALEC. Over the next six months, 30 of the bill's co-sponsors received campaign contributions from private prison lobbyists or companies, including CCA and The GEO Group. (30)

It was no surprise that Arizona politicians passed this law because not only are they receiving money, but they could assure private prisons an occupancy rate of 100% since "three Arizona for-profit prison contracts have a staggering 100% quota" (ITPI 2).

Private prisons aren't stopping there, according to the same report by Ashton and Petteruti where they find, "Since SB 1070 was signed into law in April 2010, five other state legislatures have introduced similar bills, including HB 87 in Georgia which became law on May 13, 2011" (30). In this case, HB 87, according to the ACLU's "Blog of Rights," "authorizes police to demand 'papers' demonstrating citizenship or immigration status during traffic stops, and criminalizes Georgians who interact daily with undocumented individuals." Not only are undocumented immigrants criminalized but those who interact with them are criminalized as well. With private prisons creating anti-immigrant laws such as the SB 1070, HB 87, and other similar legislation throughout the country, it represents the perfect money-making machine, much to the undocumented immigrants' dismay.

Ultimately, private prisons fail to address overcrowding in the long run, as their current existence essentially depends on overcrowding. States aren't willing to privatize their entire prison system, so when crime goes down, their business suffers. To prevent potential loss, private prisons create contracts, lobby heavily, and skimp on rehabilitation programs so that the states have to rely on private prisons to alleviate overcrowding. If left alone, overcrowding would only become worse as private prison companies could potentially criminalize trivial acts. Private prisons are only detrimental in their current state, and if there should be a future with private prisons, then they must be held more accountable for their actions. Instead of just housing prisoners, they should be paid on their performance of getting prisoners back on their feet, making reparations, and being useful to society. They should also incur the risks of an unstable crime rate and not use contracts or lobbying to ensure profits; because, if a company aims to profit by locking people behind bars, then they should be more responsible for it.

Works Cited

American Civil Liberties Union. "Banking on Bondage." *American Civil Liberties Union.* American Civil Liberties Union, 2 Nov. 2011. PDF file. 13 Nov. 2014.

———. "Blog of Rights: HB 87." *American Civil Liberties Union.* American Civil Liberties Union, n.d. Web. 26 Nov. 2014.

Ashton, Paul, and Amanda Petteruti. "Gaming the System." *Justice Policy Institute.* Justice Policy Institute, 22 June 2011. PDF file. 12 Nov. 2014.

Corrections Corporation of America. "Annual Report Pursuant to Section 13 or 15(d) of the Securities Exchange Act of 1934 for the Fiscal Year Ended December 31, 2010." *Corrections Corporation of America.* Corrections Corporation of America, 2013. PDF file. 16 Nov. 2014.

Cowling, Mark. "Private Prisons Invest In Rehabilitation, But Results Aren't Measured." *Prison Legal News.* Prison Legal News, 22 May 2014. Web. 23 Nov. 2014.

Federal Bureau of Investigation. "Crime in the United States 2012." *Federal Bureau of Investigation*. Federal Bureau of Investigation, n.d. Web. 20 Nov. 2014.

In the Public Interest. "How Lockup Quotas and 'Low-Crime Taxes' Guarantee Profits for Private Prison Corporations" *In the Public Interest*. In the Public Interest, 19 Sept. 2013. PDF file. 15 Nov. 2014.

Truthloader. "Private Prisons: How U.S. Corporations Make Money Out of Locking You Up." Online video clip. *YouTube*. YouTube, 07 Nov. 2013. Web. 19 Nov. 2014.

THE PRESCHOOL POTENTIAL

Blake Doyle

Instructor: Stacey Bieber

CRITICAL QUESTION

In this essay, how does the author assert the exigency for offering a universal preschool program in the United States? In what ways does this essay's organizational structure impact its rhetorical effectiveness? Explain.

Author Statement: *After reading The Other Wes Moore by Wes Moore, which follows two men raised in similar settings yet resulting in different adult lives, I recognized education as a prominent factor. I began questioning myself about preschool and its true importance to an individual later in life. An enormous nationwide conversation about the topic has been going on for years, leaving a lot of credible evidence and studies pertaining to the subject. I decided to write on the topic thinking preschool to be an interesting topic to research because it has influence over the majority of United States citizens today.*

From the moment of birth, a child will instantaneously become influenced and molded by his or her surroundings, rendering each child unique and independent from one another. As an infant, development is highly dependent on the environment the child is exposed to and the caregivers, which the child relies upon. These factors have an immense role in the child's future development and character, influencing early skills and morals, which are the basis for what the child will be building throughout his or her entire life. It is essential for this early development to be carefully embraced and tailored in a specific way to mold one's newborn into a good citizen. Caregivers have developed numerous techniques in order to give their newborn the first push toward future well-being. Listening to classical composers such as Beethoven, massaging limbs to promote growth, and reading aloud literature are all ways to set a child on an early path towards a successful future. Although these methods are highly beneficial, in our modern American economy, the majority of U.S. children are unable to have individual fulltime caregivers to carefully tailor their social, cognitive, and intellectual growth until grade school. Instead, modern preschool institutions have filled this role for those who can either afford it or are provided universal preschool, giving a child a structured curriculum and allowing for significant growth. Unfortunately, nearly half of U.S. children are unable to attend preschool, primarily due to cost. However, preschool education has a direct correlation to a child's future success or failure therefore rendering it a necessity for all toddlers. By implementing universal preschool in the United States, there is high potential for vast benefits economically and socially.

During the first five years of a child's life, structured learning is not required by law. This allows the caregivers of a child to have various options whether it be daycare, preschool, or to simply keep the child at home. Depending on the circumstances, each of these options will have a specific appeal to each individual. No matter what is chosen, when the child turns five-years old and enrolls within a local kindergarten program, children from all different backgrounds will be brought together. However, at this point an early achievement gap among the children will begin to appear between those who attend preschool and those who do not. Many of these children, having attended preschool, will perform at grade level or higher, yet those who have had no previous schooling experience will often fall behind their more prepared peers. Although appearing minor during this time, "Kids without that early boost have been shown to be more likely to get special-needs services, be held back a grade or two, get in trouble with the law and become teen parents" (Schoenberger). In order to eliminate this gap, universal preschool "offers educators the best shot for getting children of varying backgrounds on equal footing" (Schoenberger). This early academic gap does not always determine whether a child will be a future lawyer or a financial burden on the state; however, if each child had attended a preschool program, the chances of a child facing future hardship is lessened.

It has become common knowledge that structured educational programs pave the road to future well-being and lead one away from becoming involved in poverty and crime. This often correlates to students completing high school and proceeding into a university system. Although a college education has great potential to veer an individual away from future poverty, a child's upbringing will have a significant impact as to whether a child will follow the route to college. This positive trajectory is often established at a very young age, with early education being a prominent factor. Following the achievement gap, this discrepancy follows a child throughout his or her entire life, ultimately setting a path whether it be negative or positive. In a long-term study conducted in Chicago, researchers followed several children from their earliest years until they were twenty-eight years old. This study provided data showing that "those who had attended preschool were 28% less likely to develop alcohol or other drug problems or to wind up in jail or prison in adulthood" (Szalavitz). The study also concluded that preschool alumni's "odds of being arrested for a felony were cut by 22% and they were 24% more likely to attend a four-year college" (Szalavitz). Displaying a strong correlation between those who attended preschool and those who achieve success, this economic study displays the importance of an early education. By implementing public preschool, children from low income families have significantly decreased chances of following a path towards a poverty and crime ridden life, ultimately improving "college enrollment rate, . . . and it will also bring higher tax revenues because more workers will be earning higher wages" (Heckman).

Although appearing to be a large financial burden, which affects the troubled United States economy, public preschool programs have potential to actually stimulate the economy. Due to it's tendency to set young scholars on a path to future social and financial well-being, universal preschool could be considered a long-term investment into the United States' future economy. Preschool programs also allow for the caregivers of these young children to continue to work. In France, the L'ecole Maternelle program as well as the other free daycare programs for children as young as three months old allow the caregivers to sustain a career while taking care of the children. Although employment tends to decrease as women have children no matter what country of origin, in France, "over 80 percent for women with one child and impressively over 50 percent for women with three or more children" are able to sustain a career (Lundberg). This is an enormous financial safety net for the women of France, and with its implementation in the United States, mothers will have less chances of being trapped by poverty as well as setting their children on the route to future financial success.

All children are born with a clean slate, knowing nothing except for innate abilities and emotions; however, once the child is opened up to the world, growth is continuous until death. As surroundings, experiences, and caretakers shape each child, individuality is formed, rendering no child the same. During these early years, children develop at an alarming rate, impacted by every entity they encounter. One of the most essential factors in this development is the experiences and growth permitted by early education. Attending preschool plays a significant role in shaping each individual child as well as setting each child on a trajectory to future success and well-being. Without it, children are susceptible to falling behind in an academic gap, and increasing their chances of becoming poverty stricken and immersed in crime. With countries like France showing the great economic benefits of a successful public preschool program, the United States should be the next in line to implement universal preschool in order to invest in the nation's future.

Works Cited

Heckman, James, and Lakshmi Raut. "Intergenerational Long Term Effects of Preschool-Structural Estimates from a Discrete Dynamic Programming Model." National Bureau of Economics, 1 May 2013. Web. 13 Nov. 2014.

Lundberg, Claire. "Maybe Working Moms Can Have It All—If They Live in France." *Slate Magazine*. Web. 13 Nov. 2014.

Schoenberger, Chana. "Preschool: The Littlest Job-Readiness Program?" *At Work RSS*. Wall Street Journal, 31 May 2012. Web. 13 Nov. 2014.

Szalavitz, Maia, and Maia Szalavitz. "How to Cut Crime, Alcoholism and Addiction? It's Not Elementary, But Preschool." *Time*. Time, 09 June 2011. Web. 13 Nov. 2014.

CRITIQUING CONSUMERISM

"Should colleges across the nation start giving paychecks
to their student athletes? These student athletes are
putting a lot of their time into playing the sport they
love, which cuts away the time needed to study for their
classes; these athletes are also the reason why colleges,
and the NCAA, can generate millions in revenue."

—Marcus Fadairo

GOT GATORADE?

Jazmin Bermudez

Instructor: Jaclyn Hymes

CRITICAL QUESTION

In this essay, the author analyzes the visual rhetoric of two popular television advertisements. View these commercials online. How do you interpret the visual rhetoric in these ads? To what degree does your analysis differ from Bermudez's? Explain.

Author Statement: *My experience while writing this was enjoyable and motivating. While writing the essay, I was able to write my thoughts out clearly without having writer's block and had a good pace. Due to being able to write the paper without second guessing myself, it motivated me to write more, which made writing gratifying. As an athlete, the inspiration for writing the essay came naturally. I've always found athletic advertisements both inspiring and comical, so when given the assignment, I knew exactly which advertisements I wanted to analyze.*

Success can be interpreted in many different ways. One's idea of success can be different than others because we are all unique individuals who think differently. In sports, being successful can be seen as making it to to the professional level. In the Gatorade commercial "The Nightmare ft. Kevin Durant and Dwayne Wade," Gatorade implies that by drinking their product, Durant was able to slam dunk over Wade, ergo making him a better player and more successful. The "Got Milk—Champion" commercial by the California Milk Processor Board, sends the same message that drinking their product will make one successful. The ad features a little girl drinking milk, which causes her future self to excel in track and field. Even though these commercials are endorsing different products and have different designs, they both target athletic audiences through their advertising strategies, which sell the idea of success along with their product.

In the Gatorade commercial, the scene begins with the camera focused on Kevin Durant's back, zoomed in on his jersey number while he dribbles the basketball. In the background, one can see blurred basketball players wearing Miami Heat jerseys, a basketball hoop, a large crowd of people filling up the arena, and the flashing lights of cameras. Kevin Durant weaves through the opposing team, making his way to the basketball hoop. When he is only a couple feet from the basket, the camera zooms to the face of Dwayne Wade, who begins to run toward Durant. Then both jump for the basket, and Wade blocks Durant's attempt of a slam dunk as the buzzer sounds. The scene transitions to Durant jolting awake, panting, from a nightmare. A montage of Durant working out begins: running, lifting weights, doing push-ups, practicing slam dunks, and, of course, drinking Gatorade. The scene changes to Durant sitting in the stands of the arena, drinking Gatorade and staring at the court. The scene switches to the beginning scene again; the camera is panned out so one can see the whole court, then the camera focuses on Durant dribbling as he makes his way to the basket. Wade takes off toward

Durant. Durant goes up for the slam dunk. Wade attempts to block Durant. The scene is in slow motion; the camera zooms in on the ball and Durant just barely making it over Wade as the ball makes it through the basket. The scene ends with Wade jolting up wide-awake, panting from a nightmare.

The fear of failure can also be seen in athletic advertisement by the CMPB. In the commercial, "Got Milk—Champion," the scene begins with a little girl sitting in a shopping cart in the milk aisle. A teenage girl approaches her and tells the little girl she is her future self; the teenage girl is wearing sweats, her hair's a mess, and she appears to be homeless. Her future self hands her a carton of milk and tells her present-day self to drink it. The little girl takes a sip, and all of a sudden, future girl is wearing a track uniform. Future girl excitedly tells present-day girl to keep drinking. A baton is handed to future girl and she begins to run down the aisle; the baton is then transformed into a javelin and she throws it. She emerges with a ball and throws it, symbolizing the event of shot put in track and field; after she throws the ball, she takes off into a sprint, racing past two runners and crosses the finish line. Stands suddenly appear, and there are loud cheers and flashing lights as future girl runs up onto a podium in the first-place position. She waves to her little present-day self and tells her, with a big smile on her face, that they did it. The camera focuses on the present-day little girl, who is waving to her future self. The mother, with a perplexed expression, is looking at her future daughter while grabbing as much milk as she can. As the commercial ends, the question "Got milk?" appears in white across the screen. Like the Gatorade commercial, "Got Milk—Champion" expresses the same idea that their product makes someone successful, but both accomplish this concept in a different way and allude to different things.

There are some important differences between the commercials: "The Nightmare ft. Kevin Durant and Dwayne Wade" uses professional athletes, while "Got Milk—Champion" uses an average person, who turns into a professional athlete. Gatorade's use of professional athletes hints that the product can make a great athlete even better; because to play at a professional level, one has to be amazing at the sport. On the other hand, in the "Got Milk—Champion" commercial, both girls are seen as just average citizens before drinking the milk. However, after the little girl consumes the milk, the teenage girl turns into a professional athlete. This is the same concept as the Gatorade commercial; they both show someone excelling in sports after consuming their product. In the "Got Milk—Champion" commercial's case, it's the idea of making an average person into a professional athlete and in the Gatorade commercial, it is making a professional athlete even better. Already being a professional athlete means they're really good; however, they can become better by having a strong work ethic and basically living and breathing their sport.

Both commercials use the color scheme of dark to light to subtly express the idea of making an unsuccessful person into a successful one. In the "Got Milk—Champion," commercial, the scene before the little girl drinks the milk is rather boring and depressing, which can be interpreted as dark, and the scene after she drinks the milk is more lively and exciting, which shows what the product can lead to. Furthermore, in the Gatorade commercial, after awaking from the nightmare, Durant only wears dark-colored clothing, but in the game scene his jersey is white and Wade's is black, therefore drawing attention to Durant. In the "Got Milk—Champion" commercial before the young girl drinks the milk and her future self is transformed, future girl is dressed in sweats that are dark colored and her hair is messy, but after drinking the milk she is wearing a red, white, and blue track uniform and her hair is nicely done, using the similar idea of Gatorade's dark to light. Usually dark colors are associated with negative connotations and light colors are associated with positive connotations; therefore, the color change in both commercials, occurring after the product has been consumed, symbolizes that the product will make someone go from unsuccessful to successful.

Not only do both commercials share similar color design, they also share the same type of advertising strategy and audience, and they are selling success. The common advertising strategy between these two commercials is the need to achieve. In other words, advertisers will link their product to being successful or attempting to sell the idea that their product caused this success. This strategy is seen in the Gatorade advertisement through Durant making a slam dunk over Wade. The advertisement is alluding to the idea that the product made Durant a better player, ergo successful. The need to achieve is also used in the milk advertisement through the little girl drinking milk causing her future self success in track and field. The advertisement implies that the only reason the teenage girl was able to rise from an unsuccessful life was because her younger self drank milk. Therefore, the message both advertisers send to their audiences is that if people consume their product, they will become successful. Both advertisements have an audience of athletes; however, the milk commercial extends its audience to young kids and parents. It reaches a young audience because it's implying that if young people drink milk, they will grow up to be successful. The advertisement also reaches out to parents because the mother fills the cart with milk. In other words, it tells parents that if they give their children milk, they will grow up to be successful.

Both commercials send the message of success. Although the advertisements are for different companies and have different products, they have similar ideas. Both use the strategy of the need to achieve. Even though the Gatorade commercial uses professional athletes who are already successful, they still manage to sell success by making Durant a greater player. The "Got Milk—Champion" commercial has a unique design, and the characters were average people and not anyone famous, which allows the viewers to connect more with the advertisements. However, both commercials use the same color scheme of dark and light, which symbolizes changing from unsuccessful to successful.

WORKS CITED

Gatorade. "The Nightmare ft. Kevin Durant and Dwayne Wade." Commercial. *YouTube*. Gatorade, 27 Mar. 2013. Web. 28 Sept. 2014.

Milk. "Got Milk—Champion." Commercial. *Got Milk*. The California Milk Processor Board, n.d. Web. 20 Oct. 2014.

ADDING ON TO THE CRISIS

Michelle Reyes

Instructor: Noreen Lace

CRITICAL QUESTION

How does the author use the three rhetorical appeals—ethos, logos, and pathos—to analyze the article? Furthermore, to what degree does the author's consideration of logical reasoning help build her argument? What conclusions does the author come to about the effectiveness of the article? Do you agree or disagree with her conclusion? Explain.

Author Statement: *This essay prompt made me feel a lot more comfortable than any other. In high school, my AP Language and Composition teacher had us writing timed rhetorical analysis essays, two each week. As I got more practice, I became a better writer and had more confidence in my writing. I have learned to analyze an article instead of merely summarizing what I have read.*

For many years, America has struggled to lessen the environmental crisis. In "Consumerism Is Eating the Future," Andy Coghlan explains that this struggle continues because contemporary society encourages humans to excessively consume. Throughout the article, he assures the reader that every resource must be used because humans believe that will resolve everything. Coghlan conveys a weakened ethical approach, but improves the persuasion of his article through the use of strong emotional appeals and specific logical approaches. Although provided with many opportunities, he manages to not include any fallacies in his article; this adds on to the effectiveness to persuade the audience even more. Overall, Coghlan succeeds in writing an article that convinces the audience that humans are not taking the necessary measures to solve environmental issues.

The purpose of "Consumerism Is Eating the Future" is to explain that current environmental problems are worsening with humans taking up nearly every resource possible, as well as continuing to consume in the hopes of improving the economy. He wants the reader to blame society for influencing humans to have such mindsets. Since this article is from 2009, it is possible that the targeted audience is those affected by the 2007-09 economic recession in America. He is specifically directing his article to those dealing with the aftermath of this recession because they are the ones trying to avoid another one. Coghlan wants them to see that they are not handling the situation effectively but instead are setting themselves up for disaster. The main focus is that humans are continually creating a more damaging situation for the future of their society by unnecessarily using the limited resources available and needlessly consuming for the sake of the economy.

Coghlan utilizes pathos in order to provoke guilt in the audience making the article effective. He argues that instead of making progress, society is adding to the problem. The use of assertive vocabulary is conveyed throughout by generalizing that humans are not correctly approaching environmental issues. Coghlan states that humans are "subconsciously still driven by an impulse for survival, domination and expansion" (282). In other words, he is assuring the audience that society as a whole has been influenced to believe that the only way to solve a crisis is to consume and use every resource possible. He goes on to explain that spending money to strengthen the economy will not diminish the damage being done to the environment. The emotional appeal is also achieved through the use of figurative language. A metaphor is included in the article to compare the advertising of today to construction. In this comparison, Coghlan states, "Advertising is an instrument for construction of people's everyday reality, so we could use the same media to construct a cultural paradigm in which conspicuous consumption is despised" (283). He is explaining that today's advertising influences the people to believe the best way of surviving is to continually consume. This metaphor supports Coghlan's idea to resolve this issue using advertising as a resolution. Instead of feeding the people ruin, resolution should be presented nationwide.

Coghlan's ethical appeal is initially strong, but is inconsistent throughout the article. A specific source is introduced to begin the building of his credibility; however, soon after he becomes vague. His lack of further description of one of his sources weakens his ability to gain the trust from his audience. He first introduces an epidemiologist named Warren Hern of the University of Colorado at Boulder. By stating his profession, Coghlan is establishing that Hern specialized in epidemiology and is providing truthful information. The ethos in his article is then destabilized when William Rees is presented because the only information provided is where he attended college; we do not know what his expertise is in, meaning that he could be giving false information. The same is done when Coghlan uses Marc Pratarelli as a source, but does not inform the audience of his specialty. Having said that, the reader may not be able to trust Hern because his profession is unknown. Coghlan then confuses the audience by providing information that could possibly be unreliable. His aim is to prove that if humans continue to irresponsibly use the limited amount of resources available, they will be left with insufficient quantities. In order to rebuild the ethical approach for Rees, he goes on to explain a method he developed. Coghlan explains to the reader that Rees established the ecological footprint analysis (EFA) to generate "figures that conveniently demonstrate where consumption is least sustainable, and how fast finite material resources are being used up" (283). He is providing proof that can be tested by the reader, which reinforces his credibility. By stating that Rees created this process, he is reassuring the audience that his sources are trustworthy and should not be doubted.

A logical approach is also included in order to convey how severe the damage already is. Coghlan refers to the Living Plant Report 2008 study done by the World Wildlife Fund to provide the reader with data on the issue. He effectively proves to the reader that the consumption in the United States is causing potentially fatal consequences. He explains that humans are "consuming 30 percent more material than is sustainable from the world's resources" (283). His purpose is to guarantee a loss of resources in America because society is continually using more than necessary. He reinforces this by confirming that the most consumption takes place in North America "equivalent to 9.2 global average hectares per capita" (283). The current destruction is worsening every day; humans do not realize that action must be taken to recover, which can be done by preserving the remaining resources. Coghlan effectively uses logos to convey to the audience that careless consumption must come to an end. A solution is offered in order to further strengthen his logical appeal. He not only successfully expresses that excessively consuming is destructive to the future of society, but he also lets the audience know that there is still hope. The idea he focuses on is the need to preserve what is available in order to continue growing. He shares that "North Americans should be taking steps to lower their eco-footprints by almost 80 percent, to free up the 'ecological space' for justifiable growth in the developing world" (283). In other words, more does not always mean better when it comes to the use of resources and consumption. He succeeds in persuading readers that instead of spending and using up everything available, they should keep spending to a minimum and focus on the preservation of what is left to use.

Andy Coghlan effectively persuades his reader through the use of rhetorical devices. His credibility is questioned throughout the article; however, it is not enough to affect the overall persuasion of the article. The use of fallacies could have added on to his lack of trust, but he did not include any. Coghlan uses pathos in order to productively convey that the audience is responsible for much of the damage that has been done to the environment. The use of logical reasoning adds on to the strength of the article by providing specific data on how America is already being affected. Andy Coghlan effectively persuades the audience that humans must take immediate action in lessening their consumption and increasing their concern for the resources available.

Work Cited

Coghlan, Andy. "Consumerism Is Eating the Future." *Argument*. Eds. Gooch and Seyler. New York: McGraw-Hill, 2013. 282-83. Print.

Paying College Athletes?
Marcus Fadairo

Instructor: Nicole Eschen

Critical Question

What is this author's position in regard to college athletes receiving a paycheck? What reasons does the author give to support his position? Compared to the author, where do you stand on this issue? Explain.

Author Statement: *Writing this piece became enjoyable to put together. This is a topic that I am highly interested in and one that challenged me to take a position all the way through. I enjoyed reading article upon article about whether or not college athletes should be paid and how the authors defended their positions. This was an essay that had me use many different sources, from blog posts to academic articles, to support my position.*

Should colleges across the nation start giving paychecks to their student athletes? These student athletes are putting a lot of their time into playing the sport they love, which cuts away the time needed to study for their classes; these athletes are also the reason why colleges, and the NCAA, can generate millions in revenue. Joe Nocera argues that colleges should be able to recognize that the men's basketball and football teams have become a booming business for them all because the colleges and the NCAA can generate billions in revenue from TV deals, ticket sales, etc., and since they are able to make billions, they should be able to pay the work force, the student athletes. Nocera realizes the hypocrisy in college sports where coaches can earn millions to coach teams while the labor force that helps the coaches, the players, get nothing. I can agree with Nocera on the grounds that the college men's basketball and football teams are the real labor forces that help the coaches, colleges, and the NCAA generate billions, but I cannot agree with paying these student athletes a salary.

If there were a system where college athletes would be paid to play, it would undermine the main objective of what going to college should be about, which is to get the education they need that will help them in their lifetimes. These college athletes gain knowledge and a lifetime of skills they can use in their futures, which cannot be compared to the amount of money on a paycheck. Kate Murphy argues, "the phrase 'student-athlete' describes collegiate-level athletes for a reason. Players are receiving an advanced education at universities and colleges that thousands of Americans can't attend." The entire purpose of going to college is to get a proper education and to use that knowledge in the careers they want to pursue. Even if these college athletes were football players or basketball players, they should be more concerned with their education because that knowledge will be worth more in their desired careers than the money they would have received for playing sports. Besides, there is that uncertainty of not being able to make it to the professional level. Not all college athletes will be going to the pros, so why not focus more on the education rather than the paycheck? According a NCAA report, they explain what the chances are for a student-athlete to go pro in their sport. For example, the NCAA explains that 1 in 30 high school senior boys who play basketball will get to play for an NCAA college team. Furthermore, out of the students who play for an NCAA team, only 1 in 75 male college seniors will be accepted onto a professional NBA team. Many athletes dream of making big money to play for a professional team in their sport, but the chances of that are slim. That is why they should focus more on their education. If college athletes are not able to go professional, then they still have earned the required skills to use in their futures.

Colleges and the NCAA may be making billions off of the players, who are the work force that generates the revenue, but those two organizations are businesses, and businesses need to make money. Yes, colleges are a place of learning, but these schools need to make money somehow, and if most of the money is coming from athletic departments, mainly from the basketball and football programs, then it must be done. It is understandable to view what colleges are doing as unfair because student athletes are putting a lot of their own time into working out and playing the sport when the time could be used for their studies. In some schools, their football programs consist of 15-20 hours a week of football practice. This may appear as too a busy schedule to try to manage studying and working, but these student-athletes know what they're getting into. Scoop Jackson agrees, "Yes, for the most part, colleges and universities are making money off of the backs, performances and success of major football and men's basketball programs and the scholarship athletes who play them. But ask yourself: Isn't that what most businesses do? Yes, business. Not college athletics. *Business*, man" (Jackson). The perspective of how players are being used to generate the billions of dollars, none of it going to them, is what makes many forget that colleges are also businesses. Before a student athlete decides to play for the college of his choice, that student must sign a letter of intent to accept a scholarship and play the sport. That letter basically says that the college will be making money from the efforts of that student, if he accepts. This is like signing a contract to play a professional sport. What I mean by this is that these college athletes, just like the professionals, earn money from what they do; however, they earn it in the form of scholarships.

College athletes are under-appreciated; they sacrifice so much to play a sport they love, which results the schools getting rich. Peter DiPrimio provides examples of how much money a college makes by participating in a tournament saying that Notre Dame earned $1.7 million for participating in the Sun Bowl in 2012. In order for colleges to profit, it will be up to the athletes to work hard to achieve a successful season. One can argue that student athletes are the real reason as to why colleges can make millions, giving a reason to start paying them. There are other methods to compensate college athletes for what they do for their schools: increasing the value of their scholarships so that it can cover textbooks, tuition, other college fees, and enough for any additional years so that college athletes can continue their educations. Nocera developed his own system to properly compensate college athletes for what they do, two of which I agree can be realistically achieved: "Every player who stays in school for four years would also get an additional two-year scholarship, which he could use either to complete his bachelor's or get a master's degree. That's the third element. The fourth: Each player would have lifetime health insurance." The colleges make billions in revenue, so why not split some of that with the players. If they were to put more value into scholarships then it can help with the student's education because they can properly afford the fees, tuition, food, books, room and board, and the additional years they need to further their education. A college is an institution of learning, so why not help the college athletes get the best education they deserve. Kelly Holland and John W. Schoen argue, "in 2013, the average amount of money awarded to NCAA Division 1 athletes was $13,821 for men and $14,660 for women. Other divisions offer less, and Division 3 schools offer no athletic scholarships at all." Some of those Division 1 schools include universities like UCLA and USC, and getting a $15,000 scholarship will almost cover half of UCLA's $34,000 and USC's $24,000 tuition. The lucky ones will get a full ride, but for most they still pay the other fees their scholarships do not cover. Colleges should bump the value of their athletes' scholarships since they can afford to do so.

Paying college athletes with money is not the best way to show how much colleges appreciate their athletes. Payment would undermine the entire purpose of what college is supposed to be, a place to learn, and the skills the athletes are taught can be applied in their lives. It may be unfair to have college athletes work so hard to earn no salary, but colleges are a business, too. College athletes are under-appreciated, but rather than having them paid in cash, I believe that alternative methods like adding to the value of their scholarships would be a better solution.

Works Cited

DiPrimio, Pete. "Is Paying College Athletes Worth the Cost?" *McClatchy-Tribune Business News* (2011): n. pag. *ProQuest*. Web. 10 Dec. 2014.

Holland, Kelly, and John W. Schoen. "Athletic Scholarship Costs Don't Always Add Up for Hopeful Parents." *NBC News*. NBC News, 13 Oct. 2014. Web. 04 Dec. 2014.

Jackson, Scoop. "The Myth Of Parity." *ESPN*. ESPN Internet Ventures, 12 Sept. 2013. Web. 04 Dec. 2014.

Murphy, Kate. "Privilege, Not Job: College Athletes Shouldn't Be Paid." *The Pendulum*. The Pendulum, 13 Apr. 2014. Web. 02 Dec. 2014.

Nocera, Joe. "Let's Start Paying College Athletes." *The New York Times*. The New York Times, 31 Dec. 2011. Web. 04 Dec. 2014.

"Estimated Probability of Competing in Athletics Beyond the High School Interscholastic Level." *NCAA*. N.p., 24 Sept. 2013. Web. 09 Dec. 2014.

CITY OF ANGELS: SPATIAL ANALYSIS

"The Skirball Cultural Center is a beautiful place and
strikingly sentimental and informative. This museum
serves the community as a place of learning."

—Aminta Lagos

Identity Crisis in the Space of Conformism
Jasmine Ruffin

Instructor: Kitty Nard

Critical Question

In this essay, the author analyzes Los Angeles as a "space" ruled by consumerism and conformism. To what extent is this a Los Angeles issue or is it a larger societal one? In other words, how is the space of L.A. creating a unique problem? Just as this author integrates sources to support the main points of her thesis, how might you incorporate her assertions about space as a means to further your argument?

Author Statement: *For Project Space, the focus of the progression was discerning how space is perceived in different social atmospheres. In the texts Convergences and Another City, I was exposed to different views of space and social behaviors. My essay, gave me the opportunity to discuss how people's perspectives and behaviors are altered by the spaces of which they reside. This essay encouraged me to develop a new outlook and understanding of the world from an objective lens, testing my abilities to think abstractly. Part of the assignment was to attend and observe a Los Angeles-based event or visit a L.A. area. I chose to attend the OC 626 Night Market, which is where my inspiration for this essay began.*

In this world, we are always occupying a space. As discussed in *Convergences*, whether it is a public, private, or transient space, every space has an atmosphere that people are aware of. Once de-familiarized with an area, one discovers that everywhere we go, there is an outward appearance that is considered to be socially acceptable; individuals will often choose to conform to the societal norm or deny it at the cost of disapproving looks. In every space, these appearances and behaviors challenge one's identity and can have an effect on our consumerist nature. Stefano Passini analyzes this concept and addresses how people sacrifice their identities to be comfortable and thus conform to the expectations of others. This common occurrence is very pronounced in particular areas, such as Los Angeles and is noted in the anthology, *Another City*, edited by David L. Ulin. As seen through my fieldwork and various literature works, the desire for acceptance in spaces alters our behavior and identity, which leads to conformism and consumerism.

The way people behave in specific spaces that we occupy changes because of our desire for acceptance. In the short essay, "Interesting Times," by Judith Lewis, she recounts her day in Los Angeles stating, "I jog, eat granola for breakfast, guzzle Chardonnay, practice yoga, and attend premieres. I am a walking cliché. On the other hand, I am not always sure this character is me" (6). Once living in Los Angeles, she changed her lifestyle to mirror those of the people surrounding her. Moving from Minnesota, the cultures of these two areas are vastly different, and because of this, Lewis may have felt uncomfortable sticking to her normal Minnesota routine. The idea of "playing a character in life" to portray a façade is an issue that the majority of individuals struggle with. In specific spaces, people's behaviors shift and many feel as though they must change their attitude or appearance to be accepted or to feel comfortable. In the case of Brent Staples, he recounts living in Manhattan and how his appearance had an influence on those around him. In his situation, many people perceived him as a threat because he was a six foot, two inches, tall, black man. Staples altered his appearance and behavior to ease those around him by "exchang[ing] business clothes for jeans . . . [and] whistl[ing] melodies from Beethoven and Vivaldi" (333). These characteristics are not necessarily true to his normal behavior or appearance, but because of the spaces that he occupies, he must either deny the comfort of others as well as his own, or change who he is.

The concept of diversity and individualism is highly praised in many public spaces; however, in reality, conformity is still an issue in the majority of spaces because of the need to escape the judgment of others. In "This Year in Los Angeles," David L. Ulin writes about how his family ceased to partake in Jewish traditions and cultural customs to escape persecution. In attempt to conform to society's views, he remembers "when [he] was five, [his] parents traded [their] menorah for a Christmas tree, and from then on, [he] was not taught to respect [his] traditions, not even to know them, but to shed them like old skin, after which [he] might walk bravely, nakedly, encumbered into a better world" (Ulin 260). In many public spaces, sometimes our race, ethnicity, or religious background hinders us from being comfortable. From his parents' perspectives, conforming was the only way to succeed, feel comfortable, and to escape persecution in the space they lived. In some circumstances, people conform to such an extent that when placed back into their private spaces, they cannot escape their own conformity. When Ulin was trying to integrate Jewish traditions, such as the Seder meal, back into to his family, he felt as though, "this process of re-conciliation is a tricky one, and even now, I don't know what to think. I'm not the only one; from their places at the table, my parents look to be bewildered, while my brother and his wife seem more than a little uncomfortable, as if they're not sure why they're here" (Ulin 260). This is very depressing, given the understanding that Ulin and his family moved from Manhattan, a city known for diversity, to escape persecution. They conformed to society so devoutly that their own traditions caused them more discomfort than the society they were conforming to.

Similar to Ulin, I experienced at the OC Night Market in Costa Mesa conformity to societal norms, which is a commonality seen through the experiences of many culturally oriented individuals. The purpose of the event was to "bring the night markets and festivals of Asia home" in hope of reuniting many Asian Americans with their culture. To my dismay, the event was very Americanized and the concepts that were presented to represent Asia, such as pandas, boba tea, and Pokémon, are all adopted concepts that many people are already hugely familiar. The purpose became more to find aspects of Asian culture that Americans could connect with, rather than exposure to their own culture. This is also a type of conformity because it caused cultural aspects to be substantially subdued to set-up an atmosphere that is relatively comfortable for the majority of the people in attendance. Also, profitability played a huge role when it came to planning the event because consumerism is what drives our society in many social environments.

In our society, people are constantly compromising their identity in attempt to conform to societal norms, ultimately leading to consumerism. Passini addresses the psychological aspects of people's everyday decisions: "people interact 'with and what' people expect from the world around them" (370). This means people will purchase clothing and behave a certain way primarily because they feel as though it is expected of them. These mannerisms we see from people in specific spaces may not necessarily be true to their identity, but it is the image they choose to portray in that particular space. Passini assesses how our identity holds significant meaning and "the consumer culture encourages us not only to buy more, but to seek our identity and fulfillment through what we buy, to express our individuality through our 'choices' of products" (375). Based on this concept, many times people will act on consumption impulses to receive approval from others when traveling through spaces. For example, if individuals find themselves in spaces consisting of a wealthier population, these people are likely to buy products that hold connection to upper class lifestyles to portray an image that would make them more comfortable in those spaces. Ultimately, most everything traces back to one's own perception and the weight that the individual places on the opinions of others. As mentioned by Passini, our identity is connected to space and "identity is strongly a relational concept. We cannot realize ourselves if we do not recognize others, and we cannot respect others if we do not know ourselves" (380). People have become so conscious of others' thoughts that many individuals are willing to alter their appearances and behavior to feel in positions of status or places of belonging. In spaces, people are often in contact with one another and are subconsciously making judgments and comparisons. Because of this, regardless of the space, people feel a need to make known their identity for the purpose of internal fulfillment. However, if people were more conscious of the individuality present in spaces rather than attempting to conform, it would create a better-rounded society because we would be able to be more respectful of others.

In any space we find ourselves, we are often aware of our presence and the presence of others. Undoubtedly, the connections that are made within spaces correlate with the attitudes of the people residing in that space. One's behavior and respect toward others shift when that individual feels as though his or her own comfort in a space may be jeopardized because of race or ethnicity, thus hurting the atmosphere entirely. Psychologically, individuals often let the mentality of meeting societal standards be the determining factor when choosing how to portray one's identity within a particular space. This viewpoint can be seen when observing how people interact in spaces, whether it be witnessing our consumerist nature, or noticing shifts in behavior and mannerisms. Los Angeles is a city that holds many preconceived perceptions when it comes to attitudes, identities, and concepts of space. Because of this, it is difficult to reshape and define how our own perceptions have been altered due to our familiarity within a space. Society has created standards that we cannot meet continually, therefore hindering the majority's self-identity in public spaces. However, if everyone came to the understanding that comfort in all spaces begins within themselves, the way that we interact within spaces would change drastically.

Works Cited

Lewis, Judith. "Interesting Times." David L. Ulin 05-10.

Passini, Stefano. "A Binge-Consuming Culture: The Effect of Consumerism on Social Interactions in Western Societies." *Culture & Psychology* 19.3 (2013): 369-390. 1 May 2015

Staples, Brent. "Just Walk on By: A Black Man Ponders his Power to Alter Public Space." *Convergences.* 3rd ed. Robert Atwan. Boston: Bedford/St. Martin's, 2009. 331-334. Print.

Ulin, David L. "This Year in Los Angeles." David L. Ulin. 259-262.

Ulin, David L., ed. *Another City: Writing from Los Angeles.* San Francisco: City Lights, 2001. Print.

THE BEAUTY IN THE SKY
Kennedy Mullen

Instructor: Melisa Malvin-Middleton

CRITICAL QUESTION

In this personal narrative, the author elucidates the sentimental significance she associates with an occurrence of beauty in nature. How does this author use descriptive language to convey a mood or tone to advance her point of view? Like the author, is there a particular location that elicits any powerful memories of your own? Use descriptive language to describe this place and how it makes you feel.

Author Statement: *My father was the inspiration behind this essay. He is the person who I look up to and inspires me everyday. Since I was little, he has always been my number one fan and my hero. He is in the process of writing a book because of me, so I thought the least I could do is write an essay about a great memory that will always be with me.*

I was eight years old when I asked my father why he was looking out the window that overlooked the entire valley. He was studying the view of what I saw as boring mountains and buildings that seemed very unimportant. He told me that there is great individual beauty in every sunset and that one day I will also be able to see and understand it. It turned into a tradition that he would describe to me what he saw in the sky. This day he described the sky to me as being like a fiery flame with a splash of water. Being seven years old, I didn't understand how this was possible, and it took me years of never forgetting what he said to finally realize the meaning behind it. I just thought that he was messing around with me because I could never see what he saw. The beauty that he saw in this sky was never there for me. The thought that he just had a more powerful imagination than I did was always in the back of my mind. I looked up to my father for this reason and many others because he not only taught me practically everything I know, but he showed me how to enjoy one of the few things that came free in life. The Los Angeles sky is one that is never forgotten and never recognized enough.

Every night I would sit on my porch, waiting for the time where my mom called me in for dinner. My father would have just gotten home, and again, he would just sit and watch the sky. Why? I would wonder this everyday; my tiny nine-year-old brain just couldn't wrap my mind around why he wanted to watch this ball of light that adults tell you not to look at. It wasn't until I turned thirteen that I could finally appreciate what he was looking at. All those years he took twenty minutes each day to sit and watch the sky as the color had changed. It was his time to wind down from the day at work and let loose. I asked him why he wanted to be out here when he responded that it was because it was the most beautiful time of day. Ever since, I was able to notice the beauty that was brought upon me; I could take that time in my day and watch the sunset, the one thing that I found to be absolutely beautiful.

It seems as though one can only really appreciate this beauty that happens everyday by leaving it behind. I was walking down the street of Seattle, Washington with a couple family members the winter of January 2011. The five of us bundled from head to toe in thick clothing to help from the gusting winds seeping through our clothes. The sun was just setting, and I looked up to discover that my sun had been replaced. I looked at the sunset every single day so why was this one different? I remembered back to my sunset and noticed right then that the L.A. sun was so much different, and I personally thought it was much better. The sunset in L.A. is something that you just never forget. Lawrence Weschler writes about how he explained to his daughter and wife how much he is in love with the sunset of L.A. by saying, "It's that *light*! That's the light I keep telling you girls about" (667). He was currently living elsewhere and was enamored by the light on the news channel. That was the light that he couldn't just tell his family about but had to show them in order for them to understand. This feeling that I had about the sunset not being the same was actually a realization about how much the sunset back home meant to me. It was possible for sunsets to be different depending on where you are. This was the moment that I realized I couldn't wait to see my sunset anymore. It isn't just me that misses the L.A. light. It is a shared admiration by people who have witnessed the Los Angeles sunset.

There is only one time that I can remember not wanting to look at the sunset. I was living in the Santa Clarita Valley at the time and was just getting out of school at 3 p.m. This was an unusual day because it was raining ash. It was a hot day and the flames on the mountains around us were huge. We could see them from a mile away. Joan Didion discusses the daily burn index, which is how likely there is going to be a fire. On this day she talks about several different valleys and their burn index out of a scale of 200: the Antelope Valley was 125, the Los Angeles basin was 41, and the Santa Clarita Valley was 192 (506). Now the day she talks about in the book isn't the same day in my story, but there is a good comparison because the Santa Clarita Valley is almost always at a risk for fire. The sky on this day was gloomy and the ash was so thick we couldn't breathe without a mask on. I remember thinking that there was no way I was going to be able to see the sun tonight. I was scared about the fire but even more worried that the sun was going to be ruined. You couldn't even tell where the sun was at this moment in time. The only time I missed my sunset was on this day, and I will not forget it either.

Not only does the sun create a glow in the sky right before the night comes upon us, it opens up our day with something amazing to look at. Sometimes the sunrise is earlier than others, but if you can catch that sunrise before your day has begun, it can make for an amazing start. It is a different feeling that the morning brings upon us, a calming sensation that no matter where you live, you can feel. The feel of the cool morning air touching the bare skin that is exposed to the rays on the morning sun; it makes everyday seem as though it will be the best day if you take a moment and take in the morning light. Others may not agree with the fact that taking some time to soak in the sun and admire the beauty can actually bring one happiness. It may not be for everyone, but you won't know until it is tried. There are a number of other things that can bring peace and easiness to people. The sunset is only one thing that can bring joy to someone's life.

The light can't be the only thing that is going through everyone's mind when the sunset is happening. Most people probably aren't even paying attention to this amazing creation that is occurring right above us, twice a day. It only takes five minutes everyday to appreciate what is happening. If you live in this city, there is nature around you almost all the time, but there is also concrete and cars every way you turn. The sun is a piece of nature that can make people love where they live just a little bit more. There is a need to look at the sunset every once in awhile because that is what we look at when we want some peaceful time to ourselves. I learned this from my father who was always there appreciating it every second he could. It isn't until you don't have something that you can truly appreciate it. So why not take that time everyday to have to yourself.

WORKS CITED

Didion, Joan. "Fire Season." David L. Ulin 503-09.

Ulin, David L., ed. *Writing Los Angeles: A Literary Anthology*. New York: Library of America, 2002. Print.

Weschler, Lawrence. "L.A. Glows." David L. Ulin 666-76.

Skirball Cultural Center

Aminta Lagos

Instructor: Melisa Malvin-Middleton

Critical Question

In this Project Space exercise, the author discusses how a trip to a cultural center in Los Angeles personally impacted her. How does the author's exploration of the details in this environment and the historical significance go beyond a basic physical description and end up providing a thoughtful reflective analysis?

Author Statement: *Writing my autoethnography on the Skirball Cultural Center was a breeze to me. It was fun to write and I did not have a hard time writing as I usually do with any type of writing assignment. It was fun because of all the details that I could include from the museum as well as the freeness of it all. I wrote from the heart, and it was like a free write, where I immediately wrote what came to mind and didn't pause even for a little.*

The Skirball Cultural Center is a museum that holds both the *Noah's Ark* and *Visions and Values: Jewish Life from Antiquity to America*. It sits atop a low hill surrounded by lush greenery and dark green mountains. It's a beautiful building, but the inside is even more beautiful and surprising with many exhibitions to explore. One of them being the *Visions and Values: Jewish Life from Antiquity to America*. Large display glasses surround the models of artifacts that were once used by the Jews from thousands of years ago. Information is written on the walls about each of the artifacts held in the glass. Hanukkah candles and lamps are in one section. The next section is about life and death and how it's already sort of decided from what one wears during infancy to death. A circumcision cap and dress, white in color and long in length. The burial shroud, also white in color, stands behind the glass as if being worn. The times of suffering, struggles, and persecution are noted in every corner with dates and sentence after sentence scrawled on the wall. The atmosphere is quiet, but only because there are only a few people in the giant room that is part of the museum.

The Holocaust section is the most haunting. Pictures of Jewish victims are hung on a matte black wall. It is a memorial built into a circle with a short corridor. In the corridor hangs six pictures, a miniscule number from the actual million of victims that perished during World War II in the 1940s. Two young children, two young adults, and two elderly people. Both males and females. Their eyes are full of despair, of sorrow and full of life. The air is thick. It's an area that is warmer due to the torch that is lit in remembrance and honor of those brave souls that suffered and were taken way too soon because of the blatant hatred and ignorance of those around them. The most striking thing in the museum is this section where those portraits of the victims are only "six of six million."

The Skirball Cultural Center is a beautiful place and strikingly sentimental and informative. This museum serves the community as a place of learning. It serves as a highly educational space for those who have placed an interest in learning about the history of Jews.

Even for those who are not as informed, it is the best place to learn so much about the history of the Jews, from their origins to today. Their history, from the very beginning, is one of the most riveting and a true examples of strength and perseverance. Initially, seeing the first display I wasn't expecting much. Going from display to display and progressing from one side of the room to the other, my interest was greatly enlarged, seeing how they were persecuted in every single place and how they still kept going and becoming bigger people than their enemies, always striving for the best and always persevering through all the obstacles they were thrown.

They've been the strongest of people that I've ever learned about. I was able to explore the museum alone mostly, but for about 3 visitors that did not stay for long, and that was the best way I was able to take so much information in and see each display for as long as I wanted to. It was one of the best experiences I've had in a museum before and I will definitely be visiting the Skirball Cultural Center again.

ARGUMENTS IN SCIENCE
AND TECHNOLOGY

"By sending people to Mars, we would increase our knowledge
of space flight, Mars itself, and new inventions and theories
will arise while scientists conduct research for the mission."

—Becky Flores

Life after Death

Soledad Tlamasico

Instructor: Andzhela Keshishyan

Critical Question

In this essay, the author grapples with the concept that people can become immortal through maintaining their identities in social media sites after they have physically died. How does the author use evidence to develop and support the argument in this essay? What solutions does the author offer?

Author Statement: *"Life after Death" was a very difficult piece for me to write, yet I found true meaning throughout my research. The research I conducted helped me develop my ideas and most importantly my opinion on whether online immortality will benefit this generation positively or negatively. I honestly had not realized before this essay that immortality really does exist online. Simply the thought of being able to live on through my social media accounts after death is frightening but fascinating.*

Immortality is a topic that many have questioned for centuries. On Earth all living organisms die eventually. In recent years, social networking has contributed to the theory of immortality drastically. Many of the population on earth today personally chooses to create online profiles that depict their real life identities. After online users pass away, their virtual profiles are still online. They technically still exist because their memories and thoughts still exist. Online users are leaving a virtual footprint for those in the future so that these people can refer back to the profiles of the deceased and see their last thoughts or what they were like online, and perhaps the observers can relate that to how the departed actually were in real life. Although many argue that people cannot be immortal, it is in fact true that online identities do not die when the user dies in real life. Digital identity is simply a virtual representation of the user that still exists even after death if one chooses; therefore, we are already living in the age of immortality.

Research on virtual immortality has already begun to go beyond maintaining users' online profiles and into preserving a person's consciousness online. In the NOVA ScienceNOW episode, "Can We Live Forever?" host Neil deGrasse Tyson talks with computer scientist Jason Lee, who wants to build virtual versions of ourselves that look, act, and talk like real people that will live even after death. At the University of Illinois in Chicago, he used himself as a guinea pig and created an avatar of himself on a computer to preserve his thoughts, memories, and even appearance for eternity. His avatar looks very similar to his real self. He has created and answered questions that his avatar answers with his real voice. Jason Lee's research, as of today, seems to project a virtual immortality. With the help of Lee and his colleagues, the human population will have endless access to information about the deceased. The internet allows similar access to the online profile account of a deceased user. That account still depicts the real life persona the individual once had even after this person passed away.

The internet today allows users to leave behind their digital legacy after their death. Jenny Kleeman shares the story of Lawrence Darani, who was a DeadSocial mentor. In 2012, "doctors told him his lung condition was incurable and gave him only two years to live." Darani, as Kleeman continues, was "at ease . . . because he's going to be immortal." He signed up to DeadSocial, which, according to founder James Norris, is "a social enterprise specializing in digital end of life planning." It is "a free online service that lets people live on through their social media accounts;" additionally, people are free to have posts publicized "up to 999 years into the future" (Kleeman).

This generation has evolved drastically since internet usage has expanded. The entire nation has the opportunity to be immortal after their biological deaths. It may be "creepy" to adapt to this new age of immortality, but for some, it may feel easier to deal with the entire grievance process when they have recently lost loved ones. For example, Lucy Darani was interviewed after her husband Lawrence Darani passed away. Lucy claimed, "It's helping me to carry on. I don't feel desperate . . . I want to keep on doing things I would do as if he were alive. In some ways, he's kept himself alive for us. It's very comforting" (qtd. in Kleeman). Furthermore, she is supporting that online immortality has helped in her grieving process after the death of her husband. There are now new ways to basically cheat death with social networking. Immortality exists and will continue to evolve even more realistically as times come forth.

Every time users go online, they leave a digital footprint that can be searched, copied, shared, broadcasted, and is for the most part permanent. Digital footprints after death usually depend on whether the website is still commonly used in order for users' footprints to exist. Now there are several websites, such as Eterni.me, Legacy Locker, Secure Self, If I Die, DeadSocial, and others that were precisely created in order for the website to exist indefinitely as well as the people who signed up to become immortal. Keith Collins states, "We are, as a species, legacy builders. But in our own quest to leave our mark in the Information Age, we've begun to look beyond the finite, beyond the physical, and into the digital space." Collins supports that digital technology has evolved far beyond death. In this century, life as we know it can be digitally eternal.

Everlasting life is commonly desired by many (Collins). Collins discusses Martin Manley's suicide. Manley committed suicide for several reasons, including the fact that he did not want to grow any older, he did not want to be forgotten after his death, and he wanted to leave his own personal dent on this earth (Collins). Collins continues to discuss how Manley had no children but found an alternative option that appeared to satisfy his existence goals after his death. This of course was his decision to commit suicide. His actions are still very disturbing because it's hard to possibly agree with Manley since every breath anyone takes is more valuable than living digitally online. That is where the desperation of wanting to live forever and wanting to be remembered seriously impacts numerous citizens. Manley wanted to be immortal, and what is sad is that he thought the most reasonable way of doing that was to kill himself. Life is not a game; whether you live it online or in real life, they both matter, but only one is truly worth living for.

Social media sites have already been granting people immortality since the beginning of online profiling. Without even noticing it, our personal online accounts, blogs, and websites all can be used as historical background information. For instance, anyone may freely be a photographer, a reporter, or maybe even a journalist, and if many were to express and explain their opinions toward the economy, their comments could be used as a possible resource for future generations. *The Postmortal* is a story that portrays a pre-apocalyptic world where citizens have the right to consume the cure for ageing. In *The Postmortal*, author Drew Magary writes the whole story in the form of blog posts published by the main character, John Farrell. This distinctive way of writing a book full of blog posts instead of chapters is meant to show that social media is very actively used during the era in which the book takes place. Indeed, this novel is only science fiction; nevertheless, one day in the future, others may read our generation's blogs so that they may have an insight into what many felt throughout this time era.

Conversely, there are many negative effects digital immortality may bring forth. Admittedly, the future is unpredictable. In the end, the internet and the whole idea of immortality may never in fact become a real life accomplishment. Yet, there are high hopes that all the new advanced technology along with all the websites that are barely beginning to be published to the public's eye will have successful usage many years from now. The downside of striving for immortality is that people fear death so much that they are now going to grow more worried about how to represent themselves online after death instead of living out their lives with no worries. In the end, we cannot live forever, but we are attempting to build an immortal digital presence.

People die every day, but their spirits and lives should not be forgotten if that is what they desire. With all the new technology, people who have easy access to the internet also have access to digital immortality. Experimentation around the world is focusing on other methods for humans to actually live a longer and healthier life. Today, life after death can now be immortal through the internet, which is still a very advanced way to preserve memories, thoughts, and appearances. Social networking in this century has made the online generation immortal for futuristic acknowledgement. In the near future, death, grief, and remembrance will change forever.

Works Cited

"Can We Live Forever?" Host Neil deGrasse Tyson. *NOVA ScienceNOW*. PBS. 26 Jan. 2011. Web. 24 Mar. 2015.

Collin, Keith. "Is It Possible to Achieve Immortality Online?" *Slate*. 20 Aug. 2013. Web. 12 Apr. 2015.

Fast Company Staff. "Is the Web Our Path to Immortality?" *FastCoLabs*. 21 Aug. 2013. Web. 12 Apr. 2015.

Kleeman, Jenny. "Web Immortality: The Social Media Sites That Keep You Alive in the Digital World." *The Guardian*. 07 June 2014. Web. 03 May 2015.

Magary, Drew. *The Postmortal*. New York: Penguin, 2011. Print.

Norris, James. "About Us." *DeadSocial*. Web. 29 Mar. 2015.

THE SECOND SMALL STEP FOR MAN
Becky Flores

Instructor: Terri Silverberg

CRITICAL QUESTION

To what degree does this author construct a plausible and convincing argument in this essay? How does the use of logical reasoning and the consideration of counterargument strengthen the author's thesis?

Author Statement: *I am an Astrophysics major, and when given the opportunity, I love to talk about space with other people. Sending people to Mars is a dream that NASA is trying to turn into a reality. In this essay, I focused on two problems I believe must be improved in order to make a manned mission to Mars successful.*

On July 20, 1969, Neil Armstrong was the first man to step foot on the Moon. This memorable moment in history made many proud to be United States citizens. The famous quote, "That's one small step for man, one giant leap for mankind," inspired many people by showing that we can accomplish the impossible. At first, putting a man on the Moon seemed absurd, but we were able to overcome technological obstacles and achieve our goal. However, the Moon should not be the last place Americans set foot in space; we should go further. The next small step for man should be to step on Mars; however, many obstacles are in the way that make this dream difficult to take on. For example, technology is not advanced enough to support a long mission to Mars, and without the proper technology, sending people is dangerous. Therefore, the United States should increase funding to combat the health risks that come with planning a successful and efficient mission to Mars.

Any mission into space is treacherous. There are many threats that must be considered before putting a human life on the line. Every twenty-six months, Mars is at its closest to Earth, called "opposition." Dr. Tony Phillips, production editor of Science@NASA, states that although this would be an ideal time to travel to Mars, the distance during this time is roughly 92 million kilometers and estimated to take 150–300 days to travel from Earth to Mars ("The Opposition"). During this time, astronauts would be exposed to high levels of cosmic radiation if the spacecraft is not protected appropriately. Being in space for a long period would increase the risk of travelling through a solar flare. Spending an extensive amount of time in space would also decrease bone mass. Many risk factors must be taken into consideration while designing the spacecraft, to ensure the safety of the passengers.

While traveling through space, astronauts will be exposed to solar and cosmic radiation. The side effects of solar radiation include eye diseases, skin cancer, and a weakened immune system that can give way to infectious diseases. The effects of cosmic radiation are more severe because they cause cancer in most organs. Francis Cucinotta, a radiation expert at the University of Nevada, Las Vegas says, "The tumors that cosmic radiation make are more aggressive than what we get from other radiation" (qtd. in "Can Space"). A spacecraft can be shielded from solar radiation, but because cosmic radiation moves faster, it is harder to stop; therefore, the spacecraft would require additional protection.

A proposed solution suggests, "One way to reduce astronauts' exposure to galactic cosmic rays could be to send them to space only during the peak of the sun's natural 11-year solar cycle" ("Can Space"). During this time, radiation from the sun blows against cosmic rays, which will reduce astronauts' exposure. However, while we may reduce the amount of cosmic radiation, going during this time is still dangerous because of solar flares that occur during this cycle. Dr. Hadley Cocks says that an alternative solution would be to use "superconducting coils . . . to produce a magnetic shield capable of giving protection not only against solar flare radiation, but also even against galactic radiation" (1). This proposes creating a magnetic field around the spacecraft to shield against both types of radiation. However, the cost of coil shielding is about "2,740,898 Euros," estimated to be three million U.S. dollars ("Space Radiation"). Increased space funding would help reduce the severe cancer risks astronauts will encounter on a long mission to Mars by improving a rocket's shielding from radiation.

Decreasing the travel time in space is necessary to reduce the loss of bone mass. In order to do this, propulsion systems need to be improved to where they can be efficient, economical, and lightweight. The propulsion system is responsible for lifting the rockets out into space. Using fuel to propel a spaceship to Mars is expensive, heavy, and takes up a lot of cargo space. Currently, Bill Steigerwald, a science writer for NASA, says, "launch costs are about $10,000 per pound." He also explains that a solution to this would be to use an antimatter propulsion system. Antimatter has reversed properties of matter. While matter has electrons, antimatter has anti-electrons with a positive charge; therefore, scientists call them positrons (Steigerwald). When matter and antimatter come in contact, they produce an immense amount of energy (Steigerwald). The energy used will come from the positrons, which is a better alternative than using nuclear reactors (nuclear power) to propel a rocket (Steigerwald).

Although nuclear power decreases travel time and provides enough power to sustain a three-year mission to Mars, it is more complex, and more can go wrong during the mission. Another problem with nuclear reactors is that they are radioactive and there is a risk of them exploding while launching (Steigerwald). As Steigerwald explains, antimatter provides the same benefits of nuclear power, minus the problems. However, according to research by Dr. Gerald Smith, to produce antimatter, "a rough estimate to produce the 10 milligrams of positrons needed for a human Mars mission is about 250 million dollars using technology that is currently under development" (qtd. in Steigerwald). Although the cost seems high, Steigerwald claims that one must consider the current launch cost of $10,000 per pound. The average space shuttle weighs 4.5 million pounds, which means it would cost $4.6 billion ("Shuttle Basics"). However, if current technology were to advance, the cost to produce positrons would decrease (Steigerwald).

Many would argue that the mission overall is too expensive and therefore impossible. Instead of spending billions of dollars on a manned mission to Mars that may not even be successful, they say we should invest that money into fixing society's problems instead, such as improving traffic in Los Angeles or the California drought. In addition, since many risks are involved, there is a high chance that the mission will not be successful and a waste of time and money, not to mention that many American lives are on the line. Others say that we are still in our infancy in technological advancement and that the dream of sending people to Mars should be put off until we have advanced enough to make the mission possible and safer.

Sending people to Mars is expensive, but there are ways to help reduce the costs of rockets by having private companies take on the task of building space shuttles. Companies such as SpaceX and Boeing have contracts with NASA to manufacture rockets that will send manned missions to the International Space Station. In an interview with Elon Musk, CEO of the private company SpaceX, Ross Andersen explains that SpaceX "makes its rockets from scratch at its Los Angeles factory, and it sells rides on them cheap." SpaceX builds its own parts rather than buying them elsewhere, which reduces the costs. Elon Musk has a bigger plan to make life "multi-planetary" (Andersen). The contract with NASA will give him the opportunity to show that he can improve space flight, and the funding and reputation he will need to send people to Mars. To keep costs minimal, he is working on a reusable rocket that will be used to transport people (Andersen). Instead of having to spend more money to rebuild rockets for missions, Andersen says Musk wants to use reusable rockets that can come back safely to reduce the cost dramatically.

By sending people to Mars, we would increase our knowledge of space flight, Mars itself, and new inventions and theories will arise while scientists conduct research for the mission. Sending people to Mars will not be a waste of time even if it is not successful, because there would still be a lot that we would learn from our mistakes. Although people's lives are at risk, many people would jump at the opportunity to go to Mars knowing that it is risky. A mission to Mars would advance technology and keep the United States ahead of the other wealthy nations. When we sent a man to the Moon, it was during a race between the United States and the Soviet Union. We showed that we were technologically advanced and that as a nation, we were able to work together and do the impossible. It will be the same when we send a man to Mars.

When we send the first humans to Mars, it will be like reliving the time when Neil Armstrong landed on the Moon. Most would be proud to be part of this new era in the U.S. However, in order for this to happen, we need to be able to send them safely. We need to protect astronauts from solar and galactic radiation and from the loss of bone mass. To do this, we need to increase funding to support building spacecrafts that can be shielded from radiation and transport astronauts quickly by improving the propulsion system. Yes, it is expensive, but costs can go down with more research to improve techniques and by using private companies to manufacture the spacecrafts. By increasing funding, we will set foot on another planet and add another giant leap for mankind.

Works Cited

Andersen, Ross. "Elon Musk Argues That We Must Put a Million People on Mars If We Are to Ensure That Humanity Has a Future." Aeon Media Ltd. 2014. 30 Sept. 2014. Web. 11 Oct. 2014.

"Can Space Radiation Derail Manned Mars Mission?" *Madhyamam English*, (2014). Web. 11 Oct. 2014.

Cocks, Hadley. "A Deployable High Temperature Superconducting Coil (DHTSC): A Novel Concept For Producing Magnetic Shields Against Both Solar Flare and Galactic Radiation During Manned Interplanetary Missions." *Journal of the British Interplanetary Society.* 44(1991): 01. Web. 19 Oct. 2014.

Phillips, Tony. "The Opposition of Mars." *Nasa.gov.* 28 Mar. 2014. Web. 24 Oct. 2014.

"Shuttle Basics." *Nasa.gov.* NASA, n.d. Web. 19 Oct. 2014.

"Space Radiation Superconductive Shield." *European Union*, 2014. 11 Dec. 2013. Web. 19 Oct. 2014.

Steigerwald, Bill. "New and Improved Antimatter Spaceship for Mars Missions." *Nasa .gov.* 14 Apr. 2006. Web. 19 Oct. 2014.

How Dinosaurs Changed the World
Irlanda Moreno

Instructor: Jennifer Lee

Critical Question
How does this author incorporate research to further the discussion? Furthermore, to what extent does the use of scholarly evidence contribute to the ethos in this essay?

Author Statement: *The goal for this paper was to choose a topic and write an informative essay with specific key facts. I chose to write about dinosaurs impacting history and society because I'm very passionate about extinct reptiles and birds. I felt as if I were the professor teaching the reader interesting facts and origins on these magnificent creatures who once ruled this planet. I researched almost every little secret from the history of paleontology, and now I wish to share my research with new students here at California State University, Northridge.*

Throughout history many people have been curious about what life was like before our existence. Our interest in nature has led us to finding perplexing bones that have turned to stone over millions of years and have given us clues about the past. Ever since scientists discovered fossils, they have come up with a series of theories in order to know what the past may have been like before humans evolved. Over the course of time, paleontology has changed the way we look at these prehistoric animals, but almost no other ancient organism has made a bigger impact on society than dinosaurs. As long as scientists find fossils, not only will the specimens become well known but so will their discoverers.

Our journey first begins in North America where the most recognizable discoverers of fossils were the Native Americans. Anthony J. Martin states, "paleontologists found out that the Sioux tribe of the western U.S. had made legends about dinosaur bones, explaining them as the remains of large serpents that burrowed their way into the ground to die after they had been hit by lightning." In Asian cultures, dinosaurs have been referred to as almighty dragons. In 300 B.C., the first known reports of these "dragon bones" were discovered in what is now the Sichuan province of China, which is an area known for its abundance of fossils (Martin). They believed that these bones were valued for having medicinal properties, and even today some doctors in China still prescribe ground-up dinosaur bones for certain ailments (Martin). Fossils were connected to formerly living creatures by prominent scientists of the 15th through 18th centuries. Some were not even paleontologists, like Leonardo da Vinci and Niels Stensen. In 1677, Robert Plot, who was the museum curator of Oxford, made the first known description and illustration of a dinosaur bone. However, he recognized the fossil as a possible bone and speculated that it belonged to a modern day elephant (Martin). Later, Plot rethought his hypothesis and thought that he had found the fossilized testicles of a giant Antediluvian man and gave the specimen the name, *Scrotum Humanum* (Lowell, Gaffney, and Norell). Although this dinosaur bone had been discovered, described, and illustrated by the latter part of the

18th century, nobody knew that it was a dinosaur bone and eventually the real specimen became lost to science (Martin). However, our journey into finding the first official dinosaur bone discovered to science did not end the exploration.

According to Mark Norell, Lowell Dingus, and Eugene S. Gaffney, "The first dinosaur fossils recognized as fossilized elements of giant extinct reptiles were found in 1824 by the English geologist and minister, William Buckland of Oxford University." Before it was fully described, various bones from Stonesfield, England were sent to George Cuvier who was a specialist with comparative anatomy while he was Buckland's guest (Martin). Both concluded that the Stonesfield animal was an immense, lizard-like reptile, about 40 feet long. In 1815, Buckland collected the jaws and dental fragments that matched the lizard-like reptile and later named it *Megalosaurus* meaning "Giant Lizard" (Naish).

Only a year after Buckland's description of the *Megalosaurus*, paleontologist and geologist, Gideon Algernon Mantell was the first person to name and describe an herbivorous dinosaur (Lowell, Gaffney, and Norell). During the early 1820s, Gideon and his wife Mary Ann Mantell stumbled upon fossilized teeth in the Tilgate Forest of Sussex, England (Naish). The teeth were later taken to the Hunterian Museum in London and were examined by comparative anatomists including Georges Cuvier who then concluded that they belonged to a plant-eating dinosaur (Martin). Gideon Mantell then named the specimen, *Iguanodon* meaning "iguana tooth" due to its teeth resembling the present day iguana. These first dinosaurs have made the very first impressions in paleontology history but many wonder where the name "dinosaur" came from.

Dinosaurs have struck and captured our imaginations ever since scientists discovered them. However, many have often wondered about the name and its origin. Originally, scientists did not realize that the dinosaurs they discovered belonged to a unique class until 1842 when a British anatomist, Sir Richard Owen, coined the term "dinosaur" meaning "terrible lizard" (Martin). The name is derived from the Greek word *deinos* meaning "terrible" and *sauros* meaning "lizard" (Lowell, Gaffney, and Norell). Owen delivered a lecture about how dinosaurs resembled large present-day elephants and rhinos living in an unimaginable and terrestrial environment (Martin). Now that we have a familiar name for our extinct creature, what better way to talk about dinosaurs than talking about the most popular and savage carnivore of them all, *Tyrannosaurus rex*.

Indeed *Tyrannosaurus* has been the most recognizable and iconic image from the field of paleontology. It was first discovered in 1902 by paleontologist Barnum Brown, and later, Henry Fairfield Osborn named *Tyrannosaurus rex*, which translates to "Tyrant Lizard King" (Naish). Since 1905, more and more *Tyrannosaur* bones have been discovered in the badlands of Montana. Furthermore, they were described by *The New York Times* as "the most formidable fighting animal of which there is any record whatever" (qtd in. Naish). To paleontologists, *Tyrannosaurus* has also been a controversial figure in the field of science. Ever since the discovery of T-Rex, paleontologists have been coming up with many theories of its behavior and lifestyle. The most controversial theory of the "tyrant lizard" is whether T-Rex was a lowly scavenger or a vicious hunter. This hypothesis has challenged a lot of paleontologists because it was originally stated that *Tyrannosaurus* was a hunter and was formidable enough to take down prey with its sheer size (Switek). However, other scientists suggest that due to the size distribution of herbivorous dinosaurs and the large population of smaller meat-eating theropods hunting them in numbers, this may have forced larger predators, like *Tyrannosaurus*, to scavenge (Switek). In the field of paleontology, theories that used to be controversial end up being accepted with time.

For almost a century, scientists have been puzzled with the question: where did dinosaurs come from? Before the discovery of dinosaur eggs, paleontologists once thought that dinosaurs gave birth to live young. In 1922, Roy Chapman Andrews was sent to Mongolia by the American Museum of Natural History along with Henry Fairfield Osborn in hopes of finding skeletons from ancestral humans (Martin). Instead of finding early humans, Chapman stumbled upon a series of fossilized dinosaur nests with eggs from two different specimens who were later called *Oviraptor* and *Protoceratops* (Naish). Surprisingly, the *Oviraptor* was once thought to be an "egg thief" since that is what its name meant; this was due to the assortment of eggs found in what used to be their nests (Naish). "However, several associated skeletons and eggs belonging to *Citipati*, a close relative of *Oviraptor* itself, came to light in the 1990s" (Naish 71). "By this time scientists realized that the nest found with Osborn's Mongolian specimen belonged to the *Oviraptor* itself, and not a *Protoceratops* after all" (Naish 71). Not only were dinosaur eggs found in Asia, but they were also found in other parts of the world. In the late 1990s, paleontologist Luis Chiappe of the Museum of Natural History Los Angeles County was sent to Argentina and what is now Auca Mahuevo. He found eggs that belonged to the great *Titanosaurs* of the late Cretaceous Period. These dinosaur eggs contained well-preserved embryos with recognizable skin and tissue. The eggs even showed a unique fossilization process which contained calcium carbonate in the pores of the shells (Grellet-Tinner et al.).

Although dinosaurs have long died out, in reality their relatives are flying in the sky today as the amazing animal, the bird. In the 1800s, German paleontologist Johann Andreas Wagner discovered a specimen known as *Archaeopteryx*, meaning the "Ancient Wing," which is a missing link between the dinosaur and bird (Naish). After this astounding find, paleontologists have been discovering more and more evidence that the last non-avian dinosaurs evolved into present day birds. By using cladistics, paleontologists are able to analyze the similar bone structures of both dinosaurs and birds, such as their half-moon shaped wrist bones (Botelho). These flexible bones allow both animals to have the ability that no other animal (except the bat) can do, take flight.

Before the discovery of the first dinosaurs, many have been perplexed about what life was like before our own existence. Ever since the discovery of these magnificent animals, paleontologists have been unearthing these creatures and have changed the way we looked at the past. Even for those who did not specialize in dinosaurs, such as Leonardo Da Vinci and Roy Chapman Andrews, these creatures have caught our attention with their marvelous sizes and revolutionary features; the most popular of them all being the almighty *Tyrannosaurus rex*. Thanks to these non-paleontologists, they have inspired other people to go out into the fields themselves in hopes of finding a new discovery to share with the science community. As long as scientists find fossils, not only will the specimens become well known but so will its discoverers.

Works Cited

Botelho, João Fransisco, et al. "New Developmental Evidence Clarifies The Evolution of Wrist Bones in the Dinosaur-Bird Transition." *Plos Biology* 12.9 (2014): 1-13. *Academic Search Premier.* Web. 11. Feb. 2015.

Grellet-Tinner, Gerald, Luis M. Chiappe, and R. Coria. "Eggs of Titanosaurid Sauropods From The Upper Cretaceous Of Auca Mathuevo (Argentina)." *Canadian Journal Of Earth Sciences* 41.8 (2004): 949-960. *Academic Search Premier.* Web. 11 Feb. 2015.

Martin, Anthony J. *Introduction to the Study of Dinosaurs.* Malden, MA: Blackwell Pub., 2006. Print.

Naish, Darren. *The Great Dinosaur Discoveries.* Berkeley: U of California, 2009. Print.

Norell, Mark, Lowell Dingus, and Eugene S. Gaffney. *Discovering Dinosaurs: Evolution, Extinction, and the Lessons of Prehistory.* Berkeley: U of California, 1995. Print.

Switek, Brian. "Paleontology: The Truth about T.Rex." *Nature* 502.7472 (2013): 424-426. *Academic Search Premier.* Web. 11 Feb. 2015.

Popular Culture in a Multimodal World

"For street artists who receive some form of recognition or have a following, such as Banksy, it serves as a way to beautify run down areas, a platform to showcase one's talents, and a way to bring to light unusual forms of art and social messages that have gone ignored."

—Alyah Thomas

Two and a Half Experiences
Gregory Reiser

Instructor: Amanda Harrison

Critical Question
In this analysis of the television show *Two and a Half Men*, how does the author develop and support the thesis throughout the essay? How do the topic sentences help connect the evidence and rhetorical moves back to the thesis?

Author's Statement: *I chose to write this paper for the first assignment in Queer Studies because I felt by choosing a television show, which is often overlooked for the message it sends, I would be able to create a strong, interesting paper about the topic. For me, LGBTQ representation in television is a very sensitive topic, especially considering the vast audiences who watch these shows. Stereotyping is also a big issue in the LGBTQ community, which adds to the sensitivity of the topic. When I watched this episode of* Two and a Half Men, *I knew right away that there was a vast amount of representation in that episode that supports the community.*

How or when do people realize that they are gay? For many people, it is a simple challenge of accepting it, and the challenge comes along fairly early in life. For other people, like Charlie and Alan in *Two and a Half Men's* episode "Tucked, Taped, and Gorgeous," it is a struggle to prove their sexuality to themselves, and it comes along much later in their life-time. There are common, everyday struggles that exist in the LGBTQ community, such as dealing with stereotypes, realizing one's own sexuality, and coming out, and many of the show's viewers, averaging between ages eighteen and forty-nine, are uneducated on these topics (Rice). This episode of *Two and a Half Men* helps represent and advance the LGBTQ movement by introducing and familiarizing the show's viewers with common misconceptions, hardships, and experiences that many people within the movement live through and overcome.

In the episode "Tucked, Taped, and Gorgeous," Charlie and Alan Harper both have struggles with their sexualities. They both struggle to find themselves, basing their presumptions of their sexuality on common stereotypes that are associated with the community; for Alan, he judges his mannerisms, basing himself on a "flamboyant" stereotype, and for Charlie, he judges his obsession with specialty hair and skin care products, associating himself with a "beauty" stereotype. Working in tandem with Peggy Orenstein, the female stereotype of favoring "clothes, jewelry, makeup, and . . . a handsome husband," the episode established a stereotype of flamboyancy and obsessive beautification; both of which are examples of false stereotypes (102). The episode introduces a homosexual character named Greg who does not fit any of these gay "expectations" that were implied; if anything, he was "straighter" than the two main straight characters of the show. This impacts the LGBTQ movement and helps to advance it by debunking common stereotypes that are both consciously and subconsciously affiliated with the homosexual community.

There is also a very brief reference to a common transgender stereotype when Charlie nearly sleeps with a transgender woman. The stereotype implied is that transgender women are masculine, heavyset men wearing dresses; however, the episode quickly dismisses the stereotype with the statement that the transgender woman is "tucked, taped, and gorgeous," meaning that the transgender woman successfully accomplished her goal of publicly identifying with the gender she felt was most comfortable. The transgender reference in the episode gives attention to "[the] drive to investigate . . . external aspects of sexual life and identification" and investigates this drive by dismissing the transgender woman's "male" gender, thus debunking the stereotype (Hall 68). While creating awareness of the false nature of stereotypes, the episode also relates to and advances the LGBTQ movement by introducing the viewers to the common, complex struggle of realizing one's own sexuality.

The struggle of determining sexuality is indeed a struggle; it is no easy feat to identify as homosexual, transgender, or any other type of sexuality or gender identification. In many cases, a person may not even begin to fathom a variation in his or her supposed sexuality until much later in his or her life, often occurring in one's thirties or forties. In the case of Charlie and Alan in *Two and a Half Men*, the two protagonists do not question their sexualities until they are in their mid-to-late forties. The two characters deal with their struggles of finding themselves in many different ways, just as many people in real life deal with these same struggles. For instance, Ian Harvie, a transgender male comedian, did not truly understand his own gender until he was older; he found himself in his mid-thirties. Originally, he dealt with his own struggles by drinking. Unfortunately, that is one of the ways that many people choose to deal with this kind of struggle; that example is made in the episode when Charlie attempts to simply drink away his struggles instead of facing them head on. Other people attempt to seek help, usually attending therapy sessions. Charlie does this in the episode as well, giving examples of not only the types of conversations that take place in this sort of therapy, but also the sort of denial that can commonly follow this sort of struggle. Charlie attempts to "straighten" himself out by uncrossing his legs, using simpler vocabulary, a lower voice, and less hand movements when he is talking. It is not uncommon for many people to attempt to consciously track their efforts in remaining "straight" in their mannerisms. On the other hand, Alan attempts to determine his sexuality by embracing the situation head-on and experimenting with his sexuality. The homosexual character, Greg, is placed into seemingly awkward situations with Alan, often getting the two characters closer and closer together until Alan attempts to kiss Greg, soon after determining that he is not gay after all. In the real world, many people attempt to find themselves through experimentation; in fact, I found myself through this very same method. By introducing viewers to these sorts of struggles, whether it be with dealing with the process of finding oneself, or dealing with the repercussions of reckless behavior while doing so, the viewers are given an insight into what these struggles are like and have been like for many members of the LGBTQ community. But as the struggles of self-realization are important in the community, so are the events that occur after the struggles of self-realization.

This concept of finding oneself and becoming comfortable with one's own sexuality to the point of revealing this sense of comfort with the public world is commonly referred to as "coming out" into the community, whether it be to people who are a part of the LGBTQ community or those who are not. The process of coming out can be very intimidating, frustrating, nerve-wracking, and confusing to many people. In the case of Alan Harper in *Two and a Half Men*, he does not have the luxury of "coming out" to his friends and family; instead, through miscommunication, his son "outs" his father for him. This is an incident that occurs rather frequently in the community, often revealing people's sexualities before they are comfortable enough to accept it themselves, as was the case with Alan. However, the episode deals with his coming out experience in a very comforting way; everyone accepts Alan when they are informed of his sexuality, and he is welcomed in with open arms (and often hugs) by people such as his ex-wife, his son, his mother, and even his housekeeper. The somewhat broad spectrum of those welcoming his sexuality is an example of the many different groups of people who those coming out often need to open themselves up to. It is also an example of the many support systems that people have when they come out, citing the specific examples of family and friends, and, in Charlie's case, therapists. This example of a common coming out experience that helps to further the LGBTQ movement by identifying with viewers who might be experiencing these difficult situations themselves, thus supporting and motivating those people in their processes of self-discovery and coming out to the world around them. However, there are many people who would say that these examples do not help the movement, but rather, hinder the movement.

While *Two and a Half Men's* episode, "Tucked, Taped, and Gorgeous" helps to further the LGBTQ movement with these examples, there can also be situations that might seem like they would not accomplish this. For instance, one might argue that because this show is a comedy, and since none of the characters are real and the scripts are mainly written for comedic value and the entertainment of an audience, these are not valid points that were written to assist the community. While that is true to a degree—the show, indeed, is meant to be a comedy for the comfort and enjoyment of common viewers—that does not mean that the show's content could help to identify with and educate many of the show's viewers. There are many different interpretations of the show's content, and while many are simply for comedic value, there are also lessons to be learned and themes to be acknowledged hidden within the context of the episode, and in this case, it is not hidden at all, but rather made the main focal point of the full episode. One might also say that this is not helpful to the LGBTQ movement because, while both of the characters go through these struggles, neither one ends up identifying themselves as a true homosexual. It is true that both of the characters, at the very end of the episode, do not identify as homosexual, but just because they do not identify as homosexual does not mean that they cannot go through the same struggles. There are many people in the world who experience the same thing and then decide that they do not actually identify within the LGBTQ movement after all, and this episode is an example that can fit with those people as well. Just because the two characters are not gay does not mean that there are not valid points being made that help advance the movement.

Whether dealing with stereotypes of the LGBTQ community, realizing and accepting one's own sexuality, or revealing one's newly found sexuality to the world around them, there are valid points made in *Two and a Half Men's* episode, "Tucked, Taped, and Gorgeous" that help advance the LGBTQ movement by introducing and educating viewers. It helps people realize that many people are "gay in their own way," and the struggles they go through to realize it are not as uncommon as they might believe.

WORKS CITED

Hall, Donald E. "Who and What Is "Queer"?" *QueerTheories*. Houndsmills, Basinstroke, Hampshire: Palgrave Macmillan, 2003. 51-81. Print.

Harvie, Ian. Ian Harvie: Guest Speaker. California State University, Northridge, Northridge. 09 Sept. 2014. Speech.

Lorre, Chuck. "Tucked, Taped, and Gorgeous." *Two And a Half Men*. N.d. Television.

Orenstein, Peggy. "What's Wrong with Cinderella?" *Composing Gender*. Ed. Rachael Groner and John F. O'Hara. Boston: Bedford/St. Martin, 2014. 99-109. Print.

Rice, Lynette. "Ratings Alert." *EW.com*. Entertainment Weekly, 15 Mar. 2011. Web. 25 Sept. 2014

Who the Heck Is Banksy?

Alyah Thomas

Instructor: Elizabeth Jurgensen

Critical Question

In this essay, the author discusses the terms "street art" and "graffiti" and the social implications therein. How does the author's explication of these terms' connotative and denotative aspects contribute to developing her argument? From your perspective, in what ways do these two expressions overlap, and how do they differ? After reading this essay, how would you classify Banksy's paintings? Why?

Author Statement: *I had the most fun I have ever had writing as I was working on this piece. It didn't start that way though. When we first received the prompt, I read it over and over again, unable to come up with something that I actually wanted to write about. I started thinking about some of the parks around my hometown and specifically one in Berkeley, CA named People's Park came to mind, which is riddled with some amazing street art. I was excited to write about street art and to use Banksy as my main focus as I have taken an art history course where his work was brought up, and I am slightly obsessed with him. Being able to write about something that I am genuinely interested in is what made me so passionate about this piece and my passion for it is why I feel confident enough to submit it to be considered for* Wings.

Art is subjective. What one person may find moving and revolutionary, may not have the same effect on another person. In most circumstances, art remains confined to galleries, museums, and private collections. However, in the last three to four decades, art has begun to migrate from traditional canvases and holding rooms to the sides of buildings, abandoned trains, industrial shipping crates, and many other unconventional places. Whether commissioned or not, the art is popping up everywhere, but unfortunately, there is often a negative connotation and association linked to the art, and it is covered up by building owners because of city officials. Despite the many amateur attempts at street art, there is a culture hidden beneath all the spray-paint cans and grungy alleyways, a culture that should not be ignored or overlooked. These artists are paving the way for the rest of the culture and pushing for acceptance among society. In the majority of situations, street art is covered up and removed from public spaces because it is considered "vandalism" in terms of criminal activity and violates city codes or laws. For street artists who receive some form of recognition or have a following, such as Banksy, it serves as a way to beautify run down areas, a platform to showcase one's talents, and a way to bring to light unusual forms of art and social messages that have gone ignored.

People often try to argue that street art is better than graffiti or that graffiti should be covered up and street art left alone. But when you take the time to look at them, the two words are interchangeable and have similar definitions. Graffiti is defined by the *Oxford Dictionaries* as "writing or drawings scribbled, scratched, or sprayed illicitly on a wall or other surface in a public place," and street art is defined in *Artzine* as "any art developed in public spaces" ("graffiti," def.). The "Art Terms: Street Art" article in *Artzine* goes on: "The term can include traditional graffiti artwork, as well as, stencil graffiti, sticker art, wheatpasting and street poster art, video projection, art intervention, guerrilla art, flash mobbing and street installations." In many scenarios, street art is seen as the better of the two, it does not have a negative connotation, it is often commissioned, and can avoid getting covered up. Whereas the term graffiti is often used when referring to the pieces you see scrawled on highway overpasses and on-ramps or hidden in large water drain- ing systems and typically associated with criminal activity. Alison Young examines, "the encounter between the criminal law and the uncommissioned word or image in public space" (298). She describes graffiti as the "deviant aesthetic intervention in urban space" and street art as "certain kinds of artwork or artistic practices in public space" (298). She explains about the cultural responses to graffiti/street art. Despite the stigma society puts on graffiti, it does not matter who put it up or what it is; illicit art put up on a public space without permission is illegal. However, the legality raises a question: if the art is not of- fensive or bothersome to anyone, then why take it down, especially if the art has a social message?

As for street artists giving meaning to their work, one of the best and well-known ex- amples is a European man who goes by the name of Banksy to keep his real identity hid- den. Emerging onto the scene in Bristol, England in the 1980s, his work is globally some of the most well-recognized and credible street art. Working anonymously to the public, he is known for using his art to advocate a message. His message and art is usually placed at a specific time and location that will provoke the most thought and interest from the public. It wasn't until 2005 that he became well known worldwide. Will Ellsworth-Jones, the former chief reporter and New York correspondent for the *Sunday Times*, described Banksy's launch onto the global radar:

> "In August, he arrived in Israel, where he painted a series of images on the West Bank's concrete wall, part of the barrier built to try and to stop suicide bombers. Images of a girl clutching balloons as she transported to the top of the wall, two stenciled children with bucket and spade dreaming of the beach; and a boy with a ladder propped up against the wall were poignant meditations in escape." (Ellsworth-Jones 2)

His "poignant" message of "escape" was displayed at a time and place in the world that was already under the watch of the rest of humanity. He was displaying his message of "escape" not only to the people of Israel, but to the rest of the world watching the terror and misery helplessly from the sidelines.

Banksy is also known for his installations. In the early 2000s, Banksy made his way to the United States for the first time, and in Los Angeles he did an installation titled "Barely Legal" that included an elaborately painted elephant. As animal rights activist groups were outraged by the treatment of the pachyderm, he gave a speech about the work stating that the elephant in the room was not in fact the physical elephant in front of everyone, but it was a statistic revealing the absurdly high population of homeless men and women in the Los Angeles area.

His "graffiti" is some of the most thought-provoking and mystifying work of our time, and because he has made a name for himself and is well-known, his art is not damaged by city officials or covered. It is seen just as valuable and precious as works of art by some of the most famous artists ever displayed in the Metropolitan Museum of Art in New York City or the Louvre in France. He is pioneering the culture and rewriting the stigma of street art, bringing revolutionary art to people who may never have seen it in person in their lifetimes otherwise. He is also creating a new wave of artists who follow and respect his work. According to Banksy:

> "There is a whole new audience out there, and it's never been easier to sell [one's art]. . . . You don't have to go to college and drag 'round a portfolio, mail off transparencies to snooty galleries or sleep with someone powerful, all you need is a few ideas and a broadband connection. This is the first time the essentially bourgeois world of art has belonged to the people. We need to make it count." (qtd. in Ellsworth-Jones 1)

Banksy points out that the standard way of making it in the art world is becoming obsolete. You no longer need to submit your work to salons or be in museums to be considered an accomplished artist. You have to be a savvy individual who is willing to break a few rules.

Most, if not all, of what Banksy, along with street artists like Mr. BrainWash and Shepard Fairey, does is illegal, uncommissioned work. If they get caught while they're painting, they could be fined or face jail time. Their work is often covered up by command of city ordinances, codes, or laws that prohibit art on public buildings, and they go unrecognized by much of the community, only getting their kudos from other people who create the art as well. For people breaking the law, street art still manages to be riddled throughout major cities all over the world, remaining untouched by city workers and a bucket of blandly colored paint. Police are supposed to be the ones who investigate the "vandalism" to see if there is a tie to an illegal association or a gang, but unless there is a blatant connection or the art is on a major structure like a private corporate building, the art should be left alone to be appreciated. As officers, shouldn't they have better things to do rather than scoping the city street for reckless youth with cans of spray paint? In a study done by Jeffrey Ross and Benjamin Wright, they examined the reactions of various officers from different police stations to vandalism or graffiti. They found that from a police officer's perspective, street art/graffiti is a "less salient type of crime" and therefore is generally left alone (Ross and Wright 181). Furthermore, shouldn't the police officers be more concerned with catching the perpetrator and not covering up the art.

The reason art is covered up more often than not is because it may violate municipal codes. Even if commissioned by the building's owner, the city can request that the mural or artwork be covered up if it is on the outside walls. If it is a privately owned building, the art is commissioned and is appreciated by its onlookers, then why have it covered?

If one desired to have a mural painted on their building, they would have to go through a strenuous process to obtain the correct permits and approval. Now, someone might ask, why is it so bad if you have to get approval or permits for a piece of street art on a building? If the building is being leased or rented or is owned and taken care of by the city, then it is understandable why street art would be prohibited or covered up. But on a privately owned building, why should the owner have to go through the trouble of getting permits or permission to adorn their own building with art?

In addition to the codes and laws being exasperating and bothersome, prohibiting street art could be seen as a violation of our First Amendment right to the freedom of speech. Though an abstract form, art could also be seen as a way of expressing oneself and speech. The Amendment in the *Bill of Rights* states, "Congress shall make no law respecting an establishment of religion, or prohibiting free exercise thereof; or abridging the freedom of speech, or of the press; or the right of the people to peacefully assemble, or petition the Government for a redress of grievances." If people are not able to express their opinions on their own property that is located in a public space, then their right to speech, which could be seen as a right to expression, is being inhibited and the municipal codes are violating the first given right to United States citizens.

In any case, street art and graffiti have evolved into a culture that is bigger than "vandalizing" public spaces and breaking city codes and laws. They are forms of art and expression that can be just as moving and beautiful as anything you could find in a world renowned museum, the difference being, the art resides on a canvas inside a private space, while the other is on a wall of a public space. This difference is that the art in the public space can be covered up and destroyed for good. Even if it is commissioned on a privately owned building in a public space it can still be requested to be covered up by city officials. For dilapidated and forgotten parts of a city, what is so wrong with using art with a powerful message as a way to reinvent the space, giving it life once again?

WORKS CITED

"Art Terms: Street Art." *Artzine*. Art Republic, n.d. Web. 27 Oct. 2014.

Ellsworth-Jones, Will. "The Story behind Banksy." *Smithsonian Magazine*. Smithsonian. Feb. 2013. Web. 27 Oct. 2014.

"Graffiti." *Oxford Dictionaries*. Oxford University Press. 2015. Web. 27 Oct. 2014.

Ross, Jeffrey, and Benjamin Wright. "'I've Got Better Things to Worry About': Police Perceptions of Graffiti and Street Art in a Large Mid-Atlantic City." *Police Quarterly*, 17.2 (2014): 176-200. Web. 27 Oct. 2014.

Young, Alison. "Crime Images: The Affective Judgment of Graffiti and Street Art." *Crime, Media, Culture*. Crime, Media, Culture. 8: (2012). 297-314. Web. 27 Oct. 2014.

THE TRUTH BEHIND *GRAND THEFT AUTO V*
Jocelyn Hernandez

Instructor: Vana Derohanessian

CRITICAL QUESTION

This author challenges the objectification of and violence toward women in video games. To what degree does the author support her claims throughout the essay? Explain.

Author Statement: *I enjoyed writing this essay not only because I am very interested in sexism, but I was able to receive help from my younger brother since he owns* Grand Theft Auto V. *It was really amusing to him since all he needed to do was play the game while I took notes. I loved writing about everything wrong in the way that the video game depicted women, and I feel like this piece is one of my best essays.*

Violent video games are well known for their methods of giving the audience the option of choosing which victims to eliminate and the choice of weapon they can use for that purpose, but behind most of these games another reason becomes clear as to why they are so popular to the public. Sexism in video games has been recognized as early as in the 1982 *Custer's Revenge* game, created by the company Mystique, which was categorized as an adult video game. Since that period of time, the game industry has created women with more realistic body features, making minors want to purchase the games. Due to this issue of women looking more sexualized, Gamergate was created. Gamergate, created by Zoe Quinn, Brianna Wu, and Anita Sarkeesian, is an argumentative claim involving the video game culture. Once analyzing several games, Gamergate came to the conclusion regarding the top five sexist video games, including the game *Grand Theft Auto V*. *Grand Theft Auto V* depicts sexism toward women by exposing their physical appearances for advertisement and manipulating the players into thinking that it is acceptable to act violent or to show any signs of disrespect toward females.

A method the game industry uses to raise their profits when selling their games is to create this illusion of women having a "perfect" body, displaying them on the cover of the CD and how they present the women's physical appearances throughout the game. Jen Larsen, in the article "Women in Video Games: A Critique," clarifies Sarkeesian's position with the issue as to why women are sexualized when the percentage of players in the game industry do not correlate with the marketing method: "Recently, the Entertainment Software Association released a study showing that adult women actually make up 36 percent of the gamer population, while adult and teenage boys surprisingly lag behind at 35 percent and just 17 percent" (Larsen 1). Due to these demographics, the discussion continues as to why women are seen with small, tight clothing throughout the game and what the purpose was for including a strip club that allows players to decide on which female they want watch strip and receive lap dances from.

Violent video games are recognized for their method of giving players a mission to complete then proceed to the next level. However, *Grand Theft Auto V* gives extra bonus points when the players lure women into their vehicles, have sex, and eliminate them afterwards. Although many might argue that these are just "games" and players understand the difference when behaving in the fictional world vs. reality, it can affect the younger group of players since they are going through the phases of understanding the ways of becoming adults. Craig Anderson and Brad Bushman assert, "exposure to television and movie violence suggests that playing violent video games will increase aggressive behavior and feelings" (353). This research proves how video games can affect people's actions. Due to the meaningless "bonus" points given to players when they mistreat women and eliminate them at the end, issues can cause players to believe that these actions are acceptable to do in reality. This could induce sexual assaults, rapes, and domestic violence or other violent crimes.

In *Grand Theft Auto V*, the characters have the ability to speak on their own and have phrases that they say depending on the situation they are in. While the characters are being controlled regarding which women to physically harm or kill, they have the ability to say phrases like "that's right bitch" or "fuck you!" Though the players are not at fault for creating these character comments, the exposure to these repulsive words toward women can lead to verbal abuse without the players knowing it. Once children are exposed to these actions or words it might affect their future relationships with women without meaning to.

Grand Theft Auto V is known not only for the violence but also how women are portrayed throughout the game. It creates sexism by putting women, half naked, as advertisements, allowing the players to act violently toward women and receiving "bonus points" as the outcome for this action and it desensitizes young children to the verbal abuse of women. The purpose of video games should not be to demean women but to bring amusement to the audience.

Works Cited

Bushman, Brad J., and Craig J. Anderson. "Effects of Violent Video Games on Aggressive Behavior, Aggressive Cognition, Aggressive Affect, Physiological Arousal, and Prosocial Behavior: A Meta-Analytic Review of the Scientific Literature." *Psychological Sciences* 12.5 (Sept. 2001): 353-359. Web. 15 Feb. 2015.

Continelli, Louise. "When Words Inflict Welts on the Psyche, Verbal Abuse Has Long Lasting Effects." *Buffalo News* (1992): N.p., Web. 15 Feb. 2015.

Grand Theft Auto V. Rockstar Games, 17 Sept. 2013. Video Game.

Larsen, Jen. "Women in Video Games: A Critique." *JSTOR Daily*. N.p., 16 Sept. 2014. Web. 15 Feb. 2015.

REAL LIFE GOTHAM
Andrew Dibene

Instructor: Vana Derohanessian

CRITICAL QUESTION

In "Real Life Gotham," the author makes the argument that Gotham is being likened to New York City. How does the does the author's post-9/11 analysis shape the essay's tone and purpose?

Author Statement: *Writing this essay didn't even feel like it was for a grade because it was exciting and interesting to write about a graphic novel. I imagined this novel to be filled with color and design that had absolutely no meaning beside to make it entertaining for the reader, but I was mistaken. Every design and color on the panels was put there for a reason that had more meaning and purpose than you would expect. Batman: The Dark Knight Returns was a great introduction to the graphic novel section of academic literature, and I hope to read more like it for my writing success in the future.*

Many who have read Frank Miller's *Batman: The Dark Knight Returns* can tell you that it is not your ordinary novel with just text through the whole book. This novel is a graphic novel, which has illustrations along with text to form a conversation between the two. In *BDKR*, Miller conveys symbolism of Gotham City being like New York City in the mid 80s as depicted in the many details within the images he displays indirectly within the graphic novel. The conversation that Miller is conveying with the symbolism of New York and Gotham is how bad things in the real world can get and that dangers actually do happen every day in an urban city. Miller uses New York symbolism because it shows the traumas that were happening in the 80s at the time that many Americans could relate to or may have experienced. As Americans living in a post-9/11 world, we can relate to this novel. Miller is using Gotham for New York City because it makes the readers fear that these kinds of traumas could actually happen to them.

In Miller's *BDKR*, he symbolizes Gotham City for New York City in several different ways, but one way, is an overview of Gotham City with many tall skyscrapers, and on the left side of the illustration it shows a building that resembles the Empire State Building (Miller 41). Underneath this building, the caption reads: "One almost expects to see the Bat-signal striking the side of one of Gotham's Twin Towers" (Miller 41). In the 80s, New York also had Twin Towers, but due to the unfortunate event on September 11, 2001, they no longer exist. This quote can hit home for many people in America who were alive to witness the tragedies that happened on that day. This can also create connections with personal feelings for some readers to believe that some events in Gotham City can actually happen in real life because New York also had these same towers.

Another example of symbolism Miller employs in *BDKR* that has similarities with New York is the crashing of a plane into a building in the middle of Gotham. At the end of

BDKR, Gotham is under attack from the mutants and an airplane collides with a building that looks extremely similar to the Empire State Building (Miller 171-172). The panels show shrapnel falling from the sky, buildings on fire, citizens of Gotham running for their lives, and mutants killing policemen while breaking out of jail. The Mutants, by the way, were a band of criminals who terrorized Gotham. This whole scene has a dark message to it—Miller wants readers to know that everyone is in fear. As a modern-day American, seeing an airplane crashing into a skyscraper instantly reminds me of 9/11. Although 9/11 happened after *BDKR* was published, many readers can still relate to it. The plane crash, which takes place in Gotham in *BDKR*, has an eerie connection to New York City's tragic 9/11.

In *BDKR*, there is an anti-crime group that dwells in Gotham known as the Sons of the Batman, who were former mutants inspired by Batman to fight the crimes that Batman does not see or is not around to fight. In *BDKR*, a member of the Sons of the Batman states, "The Sons of the Batman do not talk. We act. Let Gotham's criminals beware" (Miller 102). The whole page displays to the media who and why the Sons of the Batman formed. On this same page, four people were interviewed and responded in a negative way regarding the Sons of the Batman. However, this concept of the Sons of Batman is all too real. In the 80s, around the time *BDKR* was published, there was a similar anti-crime group called the Guardian Angels founded by Curtis Sliwa. The purpose of this organization was to make citizens' arrests for violent crimes committed in New York, which occurred at a high rate (Murphy). This evidence signifies that Miller was trying to use the Sons of the Batman to symbolize the Guardian Angels to show that forming an anti-crime group was the logical thing to create in a city overrun by criminals. The Guardian Angels were founded in New York in the 80s before *BDKR* was published. The Guardian Angels and the Sons of the Batman were both in cities with high crime rates, which can indicate that Miller was likely making a comparison of Gotham to New York.

Miller creates a connection between Gotham with New York, which is made clear by the many events that happened in both cities. One of the most obvious events that happened in both cities was a blackout. Robert Klara states, "One city, one disaster, and a million different responses were the recipe for the blackout of 1977, when lightning strikes, a bottlenecked and antiquated grid, and a poorly trained operator at a Con Edison control center all conspired to plunge millions of New Yorkers into darkness." Similar to the 1977 blackout in New York, in *BDKR*, published in 1986, a prison guard from *BDKR* states, "It's a blackout—the cell doors can't be opened" (Miller 170). In the images, Miller shows Gotham in complete chaos with criminals looting the city (Miller 170). Klara explains, "The blackout of '77 unleashed a night of looting that ended in 4,000 arrests and $350 million in damages" (Klara). There is no mistaking that both cities had blackouts with complete chaos ravaging the city. Miller did this purposely to confirm that he is using Gotham to represent New York.

On the other hand, many people would say that a blackout is common for a big city like Gotham and Miller was just trying to show the city was in havoc. This could be true, but the textual evidence and the images Miller uses in *BDKR* show otherwise. Miller uses the name of New York's former buildings the Twin Towers and also displays a building to look extremely similar to the Empire State Building. Miller also "coincidently" creates the Sons of the Batman while at the same time that the Guardian Angels were at the peak of their presence. If Miller wasn't trying to symbolize New York in a blackout that happened in Gotham, then why would he display several qualities of New York before he presented his audience with a blackout that happened before the novel was published? As for the airplane crashing into the building in Gotham City, at the time in the 80s this was a practical display of chaos by Miller because he was trying to symbolize how America lives in constant fear. For a post-9/11 reader, it may seem more horrific now in America, but in the 80s it meant that Gotham was in complete chaos.

Overall, Frank Miller was using New York symbolism in *BDKR*'s Gotham City to make the reader relate to real life experiences during the 1970s and 1980s. Miller also connects images with text to create a conversation. He makes references to Gotham's Twin Towers and illustrates a building to look like New York's Twin Towers. Other great examples Miller uses to symbolize New York are events such as the blackout or organizations like the Sons of the Batman to show the reader that these events in the novel actually happened and can most likely get worse.

Works Cited

Klara, Robert. "When New York City's Lights All Went Out: Why the 1977 Blackout Remains a Dark Moment in City History." *The Christian Science Monitor*: 14. July 19 2005. *ProQuest*. Web. 21 Apr. 2015.

Miller, Frank, writer. *Batman: The Dark Knight Returns.* Illustrated by Klaus Janson. Colorist Lynn Varley. Lettering by John Constanza. New York: DC Comics, 1997. Print.

Murphy, Bill. "A Plan to Take Youths under Their Wing / If Resurrected here, Anti-Crime Guardian Angels Would Try to Get Teens to Choose Them over Area Gangs." *Houston Chronicle*: 01. Jan. 05 2006. *ProQuest*. Web. 22 Apr. 2015.

"Our Opinion: Guardian Angel a Bad Solution the Devil is in the Detail of Steve Chronister's Anti-Crime Plan, and They Need to be Worked Out before Spending Money." *York Daily Record*: 04. Jan. 25 2008. *ProQuest*. Web. 22 Apr. 2015.

ONLINE DATING AT ITS FINEST
Daniel Le

Instructor: Emily Olson

CRITICAL QUESTION

According to this author, what are the dangers of online dating? Do you think the media exaggerates these dangers, or do you think they are realistic? Why or why not?

Author Statement: *Project Web was very fun and exciting to write, as we were granted the opportunity to write about anything we wanted that followed the rubric. I found this project to be one of my strongest and most well-written essays. For Project Web, I wrote about the dangers of online dating and focused on the catfishing technique. I was inspired to write this topic because of the growing population of online dating websites and apps. I feel very confident about what I wrote and hope everyone enjoys reading it.*

According to MTV's *Catfish*, about five percent of Americans in a relationship or marriage say they met their significant other online. The world of online dating has been drastically growing ever since 2013 with apps, such as Tinder and Grindr. These online dating sites take personal information and search for connections and matches, but having your identity online is dangerous. Although the popularity of online dating may be accelerating, there are many dangers and risks it. Online dating is dangerous because with its easy access, anyone can create a fake persona, which can lead to catfishing, misguided information, and online predators.

Online dating leads to many problems such as catfishing. Catfishing is the practice of pursuing a fake persona and passing it off as if it were your own. Many people use the catfishing technique to get satisfactory needs from their daily lives. Many people take advantage of online dating sites because there is so much control in their favor. For example, authors Danielle Couch and Professor Pranee Liamputtong discuss how "using computer-mediated communication such as synchronous chat can offer users a high level of control in their online interactions" (281). Couch and Liamputtong go on to discuss the many online dating users who abuse the system and obtain information about the significant other. Using the online dating system gives the user a lot access to the other's identity, which could later be used for additional dating sites. Online dating can give the gift of a significant other, but if it goes terribly wrong, it will end up in a nightmare.

Misguided information can lead to the devastation of the significant other's feelings. Miscommunication can cause the lack of trust in humanity and creates a tainted environment. Online dating hasn't always been easy, as finding matches and connections are difficult. Most online dating sites will often have sexual predators lurking around the corners. These people will disguise their identity online to appear as the perfect significant other that one has always dreamed of but their only purpose is to achieve the goal of sex. According to Rosanna Guadango, Bradley Okdie, and Sara Kruse, "self-presentation is usually aimed toward achieving strategic goals. People tend to present and sometimes exaggerate or fabricate their characteristics in an attempt to create their desired impression. The present investigation focused on the type of self-presentation that is deceptive in nature" (643). Guadango, Okdie, and Kruse discuss how many users manipulate the system with their discouraging fake identities to obtain most of their goals. The online dating world continues expanding with new sites that promote identity fraud such as Omegle and Chatroulette. These sites tend to have the most catfishers as it has unlimited controls and benefits to the user.

Creating a fake persona can construct disbelief and cause harm to the significant other. Identity fraud makes online dating harder because finding a match is hard enough, but now we have to stay aware of those who are faking their identities. Setting up a fake identity is easier than ever; as Molly Wood writes, "To set up a profile, you log in using your Facebook credentials and then choose a few photos from the collection you have on the site. Tinder will automatically fill in a few for you." It is easy to see why fake online identities are used commonly, as the app takes control from the user. Filling in random facts to achieve a match may cause risks for the significant other. Researcher Gianna Sobol shared her personal experiences with false information and it did not end in her favor. For example, Sobol explains, "She lied some more. I forgave her some more. We fought and cried and processed the hell out of every interaction we'd ever had. . . . Was it because I was the first femme girl she'd ever dated? Was I too gender-conforming for her?" Sobol discusses how she posed as the opposite gender to obtain her goals in the online dating world. Manipulating the system is easier than ever. Online dating has many risks to it, but if users maneuver through the crowd, they might actually find their matches.

Online dating is seen as a gift of the internet because individuals can find their significant others through the use of technology. Fake identities are commonly found now through the many new protection systems in place. Filters have been added to online dating sites and now require age limits. They continue to weed out those who pose with a false identity. Although online dating may be growing in popularity, there are many dangers and risks of online dating. Online dating is dangerous because with its easy access anyone can create a fake persona that constructs disbelief and lead to predators, misguided information, and criminal acts such as catfishing.

Works Cited

Couch, Danielle, & Pranee Liamputtong. "Online Dating and Mating: Perceptions of Risk and Health Among Online Users." *Health, Risk & Society, 9.3* (2007): 275-294. Web. 30 Mar. 2015.

Guadagno, Rosanna E., Okdie, Bradley M., & Kruse, Sara A. "Dating Deception: Gender, Online Dating, and Exaggerated Self-Presentation." *Computers in Human Behavior, 28.2* (2012): 642-647. Web. 30 Mar. 2015.

Sobol, Gianna. "L.A. Affairs: Online Dating in Search of Her Wife-to-be Leads to a System Error." *Los Angeles Times.* Los Angeles Times, 17 Oct. 2014. Web. 30 Mar. 2015.

Wood, Molly. "Led by Tinder, A Surge in Mobile Dating Apps." *The New York Times.* The New York Times, 04 Feb. 2015. Web. 30 Mar. 2015.

Challenging the Dominant Discourse

"Whenever any sort of single, normal, neutral ideal is created, it automatically leaves out someone or some group. It causes there to be alienation and feelings of 'otherness' among anyone who does not fit that particular, specific mold. It also gives anyone who does fit that mold an advantage in society overall, which completely eliminates any sort of equality among all people."

—Ariana Hardwick-Jones

JUSTIFY YOUR SISTERHOOD: MADONNA, SEXUALITY, AND THE FEMINIST DISCOURSE

Amanda de la Rocha

Instructor: Amanda Harrison

CRITICAL QUESTION

To what extent does this author make a convincing argument for Madonna's role in third-wave feminism? Does the analysis of the visual rhetoric in Madonna's videos reinforce the author's assertions? Why or why not? Use evidence from the essay to support your answer.

Author Statement: *With the completion of my music video essay, I was able to not only delve into feminist viewpoints and perspectives of Madonna with regard to her "Justify My Love" music video, but also the feminist stance with regard to Madonna's feminism. Through the exploration of popular and well-known feminist camps, I expanded my understanding about Madonna's presence and role in the feminist movement, but also the influence, reach, and thus power that her views projected onto American pop culture. It was a pleasure to undertake this essay and argue the stance that not only Madonna is a feminist herself, but also that through her actions and subsequent videos, she paved the way for many future feminists to also continue to, as Madonna would put it, "express themselves."*

When Madonna's music video "Justify My Love" was released in late 1990, MTV banned it, prompting NBC's *Nightline* to conduct an interview with Madonna where the video was first aired in its entirety (Jacobs). MTV was said to have banned the music video for its overt sexual content (Jacobs). The video shows a multitude of adult scenes and it became the first music video to ever be released directly to the public via Video Home System (VHS). This move ironically ended up being more profitable for Madonna in the long run (Jacobs). Madonna understood the reason for the banning of "Justify My Love." However, as she described, she felt as though there were other alternatives to an outright banning (qtd. in Sawyer interview). Beyond the banning of the video from MTV, "Justify My Love" became a platform for feminist discourse in the country (qtd. in Sawyer interview). Madonna was thrust into the spotlight of academic debate over whether or not she was truly a feminist. However, as this paper will address, throughout "Justify My Love," Madonna goes beyond the typical stereotypes of what American feminists consider feminism to be and takes on the notion that a woman is not only able to be powerful but sexy and provocative at the same time. Throughout the music video, Madonna is completely in control; she is the one making the demands and progressing the sex scenes along. Although it may appear as though she appeals to male sexual sentiments, she is the one in charge and she is the one whose sexual desires are satisfied. Madonna's music video, "Justify My Love," challenges traditional feminism by breaking the notion that in order for women to be equal to men, they must exclude their sexuality and their own interpretations of that sexuality. The video, with its provocative eroticism, shows how women can control their own sexuality and in doing so can be sexual beings, not merely sexual objects.]

"Justify My Love" falls under the category of eroticism and is covered under the third wave of the feminist movement that began in the mid 1990s. As Leslie Heywood and Jennifer Drake describe, "third-wave feminists often take cultural production and sexual politics as key sights of struggle, seeking to use desire and pleasure as well as anger to fuel struggles for justice" (qtd in. Hammer & Kellner). Moreover, eroticism, as some feminists state, allows women to have complete "control over their own bodies" and gives them the ability to "speak about it" (Suleiman 119). Madonna's character in "Justify My Love" embodies eroticism completely. The Madonna seen in the video dominates every single sex scene and even concludes the video by relishing in her accomplishments. Madonna confirms this sexual confidence when she states that there should be nothing to be ashamed of when having sexual thoughts, feelings, or discussions (qtd. in Sawyer interview). In doing so, Madonna confirms that her video is a means by which sexual hierarchies can be revamped through a reappropriation of sexual control.

The third wave of feminism was needed because in the 1990s many college-aged women were not feeling included in the feminist camp.[Rebecca Walker describes that inclusion is still needed in order to maintain feminism and make further progress toward equality. She states, "One of the most important [topics] that we can all think about, in terms of maintaining feminism as we go forward is the importance of passing on our belief system to the next generation and that sometimes means accepting the difference in position that the next generation will bring rather than being resistant to it or fearful of it"] (Walker). Third-wave feminism was influenced by its "mother figure," i.e. second-wave feminism, and Madonna during this time can be seen as one daughter in revolt (Henry). Madonna pushes beyond the boundaries that previous feminists set, and in turn creates a larger understanding of what feminism is, thus ushering feminists-to-be into a feminism that is not complacent with the feminism of their mothers.

American feminism pre 1990s is best described by second-wave feminism, which used postmodern theory to question ideas of women and gender. Postmodern feminist theory saw the emergence of a generation of feminists in the 1970s who began to rebel against traditional feminist ideas of women's relationships to their sexuality.[Ironically, the many of same postmodern feminists who subscribed to the sexual liberation movement criticized "Justify My Love;" many feminists condemned Madonna for pandering to men's views of women and male sexual desire.]These same feminists view Madonna's music video "Material Girl" as displaying an archaic view of the female persona by visually dressing in 1950s Marilyn Monroe-esque clothing and showing a materialistic view of women by singing lyrics such as, "only boys that save their pennies make my rainy day, 'cause we are living in a material world and I am a material girl."[They felt that these types of images and lyrics pushed the feminist movement backward instead of progressing it forward. They believed that it showed women as not only second to men, but also as pawns for men to control and play with.]

Other feminists, however, embraced Madonna's empowering sexuality. In an article from *The New York Times*, Camille Paglia declares Madonna a feminist. Paglia explains her defense of Madonna stating, "Madonna has a far profounder vision of sex than do most feminists. She sees both the animality and the artifice. Changing her costume style and hair color virtually every month. . . . Feminism says, 'No more masks.' Madonna says we are nothing but masks. Through her enormous impact on young women around the world, Madonna is the future of feminism." Madonna's feminism is further established in an interview with Forrest Sawyer on ABC's *Nightline*, where Sawyer asks Madonna in regard to the banned video, "Where do you draw the line?" Madonna replies, "violence and humiliation and degradation." Madonna goes on to discuss the fact that videos are played daily on MTV where violence and the degradation of humans is prevalent, yet those same videos are not banned—they are not even considered for censoring. When asked about the sexual images in her "Express Yourself" music video, where Madonna is seen in chained and crawling under a table, Madonna explains: "I chained *myself*, though. Ok? There wasn't a *man* that put that chain on me. I did it *myself*. I was chained to my desires. *I* crawled under my own table. There wasn't a *man* standing there, making me do it. I do everything of my own volition. *I* am in charge" (qtd. in Sawyer interview). When asked to address those feminists who believe she "doesn't represent them," she responds with, "Isn't that what feminism is all about? Aren't *I* the one in charge of my life and, making my own decisions?" (qtd. in Sawyer interview).

Madonna aptly defends not only her own person but also the content and medium through which she, whether consciously or not, displays assertive sexuality as seen from a woman's perspective, and in doing so can be said to have directly contributed to the evolution of third-wave feminism. In its broader context, "Justify My Love" was a "cultural production" that was in tune with the changes that were taking place among feminists. The attacks on "Justify My Love" provided a platform where feminism in America could continue and refine its stance in female sexuality. Regardless of how she may have labeled herself, Madonna's unapologetic stance in defense of herself and her videos confirmed her feminism, a feminism that revealed contradictions inherent in the debate surrounding "Justify My Love," namely the right for a woman to express her sexuality and desire on her own terms.

Artists like Madonna and videos such as "Justify My Love" have played a role in furthering the idea that feminism and female sexuality and desire can be embodied in a single person, that is that a feminist does not have to be a man-hating woman in order to be "an equal." As Madonna shows in "Justify My Love," a feminist is capable of being anything that she wishes to be and can define her own womanhood. Her ownership of sexuality and desire as conveyed through one erotic video may have seemed radical for its time, but in defining herself she challenged second-wave feminism to reconsider its view on the role of sex and eroticism within feminist camps. Furthermore, by its release and mass viewership, "Justify My Love" widened the idea of female sexual independence now adopted by many American women who now choose to live lives not bound to roles dictated by men, or likewise, by other feminists.

Works Cited

Hammer, Rhonda and Douglas Kellner. "Forward." *Third Wave Feminism and Television: Jane Puts it in a Box.* Ed. Johnson, Merri Lisa. London, GBR: I.B. Tauris, 2007. IX. Print.

Henry, Astrid. *Not My Mother's Sister: Generational Conflict and Third-Wave Feminism.* Bloomington: Indiana University Press, 2004. 01. Print.

Jacobs, Matthew. "A Look at 33 Years' Worth of Controversial Videos on MTV." *Huffingtonpost.com.* Huffington Post, 06 Aug. 2014. Web. 11 Oct. 2014.

Madonna. Interview by Forrest Sawyer. *Nightline.* ABC. WABC, New York. 03 Dec. 1990. Web. 08 Oct. 2014.

——. "Justify My Love." The Immaculate Collection. Warner Bros., 1990. Music Video. Dir. Jean-Baptiste Mondino. MTV. 18 Dec. 1990. Web. 08 Oct. 2014.

——. "Material Girl." Like A Virgin. Warner Bros., 1984. Music Video. Dir. Mary Lambert. MTV. 30 Nov. 1984. Web. 11 Oct. 2014.

Paglia, Camille. "Madonna—Finally, a Real Feminist." *The Rock History Reader.* Ed. Theo Caterforis. New York: Routledge, 2007. 259-260. Print.

Suleiman, Susan R. *Subversive Intent: Gender, Politics, and the Avant-Garde.* Cambridge, Mass: Harvard University Press, 1990. Print.

Walker, Rebecca. "The Origins of Third Wave Feminism." Online video clip. *YouTube.* The Lavin Agency Speakers Bureau, 23 Sept. 2009. Web. 25 Oct. 2014.

ANNOTATED BIBLIOGRAPHY FOR JUSTIFY YOUR SISTERHOOD: MADONNA, SEXUALITY, AND THE FEMINIST DISCOURSE

Amanda de la Rocha

Instructor: Amanda Harrison

CRITICAL QUESTION

An annotated bibliography can be an invaluable resource in organizing research and evaluating sources. How does this author use the genre to evaluate potential source material?

ANNOTATED BIBLIOGRAPHY

Hammer, Rhonda and Douglas Kellner. "Forward." *Third Wave Feminism and Television: Jane Puts it in a Box.* Ed. Johnson, Merri Lisa. London, GBR: I.B. Tauris, 2007. IX. Print.

Hammer and Kellner discuss the third wave of feminism and how it is seen on television. Its relevance for this paper lies in its thorough discussion of the nature of this type of feminism.

Henry, Astrid. *Not My Mother's Sister: Generational Conflict and Third-Wave Feminism.* Bloomington: Indiana University Press, 2004. 01. Print.

Henry describes the generational difference between the second and third wave of feminism and how the third wave of feminism started from the daughters of the second wave. That is, we are not our mother's daughters, however, we build upon their thoughts and in doing so change the thought of daughterhood, motherhood, sisterhood, and feminism as a whole.

Jacobs, Matthew. "A Look at 33 Years' Worth of Controversial Videos on MTV." *Huffingtonpost.com.* Huffington Post, 06 Aug. 2014. Web. 11 Oct. 2014.

Jacobs depicts the many music videos that have been banned from viewership on MTV over the years with Madonna's "Justify My Love" being the first one. Madonna subsequently made money from the distribution of the video after it was banned because it became the first one to be released in VHS format for the public to purchase.

Madonna. Interview by Forrest Sawyer. *Nightline.* ABC. WABC, New York. 03 Dec. 1990. Web. 08 Oct. 2014.

The interview emerged when Madonna's video "Justify My Love" was banned on MTV. During the interview she answers questions in regard to why her video was banned and the images that are displayed. Many feminists considered "Justify My Love" to be just another video in which Madonna demeans the value of women and plays to the male perception of female sexuality.

Madonna. "Justify My Love." The Immaculate Collection. Warner Bros., 1990. Music Video. Dir. Jean-Baptiste Mondino. MTV. 18 Dec. 1990. Web. 08 Oct. 2014.

"Justify My Love" was released in late 1990 and was banned from MTV for its sexually explicit scenes. Many feminists criticized the video for presumably being overly erotic for men's pleasure and depicting women as mere sexual objects. The video is considered to have sparked the academic discussion on Madonna's feminism.

Madonna. "Material Girl." Like A Virgin. Warner Bros., 1984. Music Video. Dir. Mary Lambert. MTV. 30 Nov. 1984. Web. 11 Oct. 2014.

"Material Girl" depicts Madonna in a Marilyn Monroe-esque performance that was criticized by many feminists. However, many feminists rallied behind the video and Madonna as well, stating that she is the one performing for herself and not for men as many feminists speculated.

Paglia, Camille. "Madonna—Finally, a Real Feminist." *The Rock History Reader*. Ed. Theo Caterforis. New York: Routledge, 2007. 259-260. Print.

Paglia comments on the importance of distinguishing Madonna as producer of art from Madonna as a sexual persona depicted in videos. She classifies "Justify My Love" as an avant-garde video reminiscent of old European films. Paglia's main stance is describing Madonna as a "true feminist" who exposes the weaknesses in American feminism, which, the author argues, is overloaded with prudish stances on sexuality. Paglia applauds Madonna's theatricality and her taking on of various personas because she rebels against a feminism that denies women of sexuality and its expression.

Suleiman, Susan R. *Subversive Intent: Gender, Politics, and the Avant-Garde*. Cambridge, Mass: Harvard University Press, 1990. Print.

In chapter six, Suleiman discusses female eroticism in depth. For many years, in American society, women's sexuality was simply the object for a man to enjoy and with the birth of eroticism, women were now able to discover themselves and change their view of their sexuality.

Walker, Rebecca. "The Origins of Third Wave Feminism." Online video clip. *YouTube*. The Lavin Agency Speakers Bureau, 23 Sept. 2009. Web. 25 Oct. 2014.

In the video, Walker discusses why the third wave was needed. Young women of the third wave did not feel welcome in second wave feminism. Feminism as a whole needed to change in order to continue on within the next generation of young women.

LGBT Identity and Society
Citlali Aburto

Instructor: Emily Olson

Critical Question

What rhetorical appeals does this author use to support her thesis statement? To what degree does the incorporation of ethos, pathos, and/or logos strengthen the author's argument? If you were to build upon or modify the author's argument, how might you employ the rhetorical appeals? Explain.

Author Statement: *This assignment allowed me to expand my knowledge about the LGBT community and their struggles amongst society. When writing this piece, it was emotionally difficult for me to fully read about the situations some individuals go through when coming out to their parents. Reading and writing about the methods that are still being used, such as conversion therapy, was heartbreaking, yet it inspired me to learn more and to reach out and help those who are forced to attend. Overall my experience with writing this paper was insightful regarding how our voices do matter and can make a difference politically and socially and that we must practice these rights.*

The LGBT communities, by definition, are individuals who are Lesbian, Gay, Bisexual, and Transgender. In the United States, some states have restricted basic human rights and implemented negative strategies towards the LGBT community, such as discrimination in the workplace and "conversion therapies." Conversion therapies refer to the methods in which therapists try to "cure" homosexuals through therapy, which include electrocution, hormone pills, hypnosis, and so on. The LGBT community has made some legal progress through their movements, but recently there have been some proposed laws that the LGBT community has yet to face. Individuals may hide their true sexual orientation because of the laws being proposed. This is problematic because society is restricting basic human rights and treats the LGBT community as unequal. Some of the state's laws, such as Indiana, suggest legalizing discrimination. Another proposed law that may affect people's sexual orientation and identity is the "Religious Freedom Act" and the continuance of "conversion therapies."

The "Religious Freedom Act," according to the supporters, states that this law protects the owners' and employees' religious views toward gay couples. This law is controversial because many say that it does not discriminate against gays but solely protects others' views. According to Avihay Dorfman, a "legal principle, freedom of religion serves as an authoritative source of political power," which in this case is seen in Indiana (281). This law limits the LGBT community's rights while protecting others' religious freedoms. Laws like these allow people to refuse giving service to gay couples. Not only does this law silence many people's sexuality in order to receive basic service, but it also impacts the economy within Indiana. According to Eric Bradner, many business owners, such as Marc Benioff, would "stop their travel to Indiana and help its employees move out of state." Many company owners have taken business action to boycott this law that discriminates against people within the LGBT community. The LGBT community is being refused rights that heterosexuals have, and not only does it affect homosexuals' rights, but it also affects the economy of that state.

Conversion therapy was mostly popular throughout the 1950s and 1960s but is still around in the 21st century. The difference is that these practices, in some states, are illegal when the patient is a minor. The health risks for patients in the 1950s were massive; many went through surgery, electrocution, and injection of drugs. Although there are still conversion therapies in the U.S., current laws limit the physical damage, but patients are still hurting psychologically and emotionally. Therapists who practice this type of conversion shame the patients by using religion. According to Flentje, Heck, and Cochran, previously, homosexuality was considered a mental disorder, and that patients who "wish[ed] to change their sexual orientation should be honored by their therapists." This was problematic because people were not accepting themselves due to the pressure from family members or religious beliefs. Such conversion therapies are still being performed in the U.S., and the conditions therapists have their patients endure are unethical. In the article, "Measure Seeks to Regulate Programs for Gay Teens," State Senator Ricardo Lara mentions how "many of these facilities have operated without regulation or any type of oversight" (qtd. in Branson-Potts). Conversion therapies being performed have a serious health risk for minors being placed in them. The threat of these may cause teens to hide their sexual identity so they won't have to attend these therapies.

Laws and methods that are used to "cure" homosexuality limit people's basic human rights and discriminate against who they truly are. The people within the LGBT community should not have to feel ashamed, silenced, or fear to be who they are because of society's laws. It is important for those who support LGBT individuals to advocate for and with them. Being involved in politics such as writing to one's local representatives about LGBT issues may help to achieve an equality for people in the LGBT community. Such actions like boycotting, protesting, informing and advocating together, on the current issues the LGBT community faces, are a step toward equality.

Works Cited

Bradner, Eric. "Pence Defends 'Religious Freedom' Law." *CNN*. Cable News Network, 30 Mar. 2015. Web. 10 Apr. 2015.

Branson-Potts, Hailey. "Measure Seeks to Regulate Programs for Gay Teens." *Los Angeles Times*. Los Angeles Times, 27 Mar. 2015. Web. 10 Apr. 2015.

Dorfman, Avihay. "Freedom of Religion." *Canadian Journal Of Law & Jurisprudence* 21.2 (2008): 279-319. *OmniFile Full Text Mega (H.W. Wilson)*. Web. 11 Apr. 2015.

Flentje, Annesa, Nicholas C. Heck, and Bryan N Cochran. "Experiences of Ex-Ex-Gay Individuals in Sexual Reorientation Therapy: Reasons for Seeking Treatment, Perceived Helpfulness and Harmfulness of Treatment, and Post-Treatment Identification." *Journal of Homosexuality*, 61.9 (2014): 1242-1268. Web. 11 Apr. 2015.

Michelson, Noah. "11 Ridiculous, Strange, and Terrifying Gay Conversion Therapy Methods for 'Curing' Homosexuality." *The Huffington Post*. TheHuffingtonPost.com, 01 Nov. 2011. Web. 15 Apr. 2015.

Half-Naked White Men
Sally Hernandez

Instructor: Nicole Eschen

Critical Question

In this persuasive essay, the author addresses the negative ramifications of stereotyping toward and within the LGBTQ community. To what extent does this author integrate the concepts of audience, purpose, and tone as a means to further the argument? Explain.

Author Statement: *Queer Studies really opened my eyes to taboo issues rarely discussed in society that happen within the LGBTQ community. Discrimination, judgment, acceptance, and difficulty finding one's identity were all major topics we discussed during class. My essay is about my experience in a gay club. My views and experiences really helped me decide what the best discussion would be to grab my reader's attention. That being said, I enjoyed writing and researching this essay, so I hope you enjoy reading it.*

Many might picture gay clubs to be filled with barely clothed men all on top of each other dirty dancing. That is not true. Right? The stereotypes that all gay men are white, flamboyant, dress in skimpy clothing, or have a little sass in their walk is not only an issue on the streets; it may also be carried into the gay-club scene, a space where there should be absolutely no stereotyping or assumptions. On my venture out to the club with my group, I was expecting it to look like a stereotypical gay club and that is exactly what we all walked into. A way to make the gay clubs friendlier and more utopic would be to make it more open to every kind of gay man out there: the "macho" gay man, the "feminine" gay man, and any other "type" of gay man; all should feel welcome and comfortable in an environment that encourages self-expression, diversity, and equality for the LGBTQ community.

Recently, I was intrigued by what I would find on the internet if I looked up "gay clubs," but before I clicked search, I put myself in the exact mindset that I talked about in the previous paragraph: stereotyping. I thought about these specific events and what I would assume gays would look like or the type of people that would attend, then I clicked search. Surprisingly, that is exactly what I found: a typical stereotype of what a gay guy would look like in a gay club. About every picture I saw on club websites were of men on stripper poles oiled up and shirtless. Although I am not saying this should be forbidden in gay clubs, I am merely suggesting that if the LGBTQ community is striving for equality and trying to reduce the stereotyping of gay men, then these clubs should mix in different looks other than a muscle man with oily skin dancing on a pole while wearing a G-string.

Priyank Jindal exposes the rarely seen segregation that takes place within the LGBTQ community. She states that after the attack on 9/11, "the gay 'community' . . . embraced New York Mayor Rudolph Giuliani without any interrogation of how racist policies have affected people of color" (Jindal 39). The mainstream gay movement fails to support the people of color of the LGBTQ community and the struggles they endure because they are of lower-economic classes and of color. People of color are pushed aside while the mainstream gay image flourishes.

During my internet search of gay clubs, mostly all of the promotional flyers had a specific kind of guy on the cover: white and over-the-top. Being flamboyant and enjoying wearing make-up is not something that should be looked down on, but it does affect the way people think gay men should look when that is the primary kind of guy that gay clubs promote. Self-expression is an important part of life, but there also needs to be a variety a men portrayed at these gay clubs. For example, white feminine guys are absolutely acceptable but maybe a black man or an Asian man that looks like he should be on the cover of *GQ* magazine will be a pleasant change. This kind of variety will attract a much more diverse crowd and create an even more amazing party atmosphere. Because club goers have different preferences, having more than one race will allow for a better experience.

Assumptions surface that the "promotional flyer" type of gay men, believed to be the only ones that seem to frequent these clubs, are the only gay men in existence. Those unfamiliar with the diversity in the LGBTQ community feel this way because clubs mainly focus on one image: the white male stripper image. Even though this image is what makes gay clubs distinct and unique from heterosexual clubs, some variation in what is presented as being attractive should take place. By only allowing mostly white males to be the performers in clubs and having limited men of color, clubs are portraying that only this distinct group of men is considered glamorous. I say spice it up, throw different flavors in the pot; no one wants bland soup.

When I was investigating the photos of "gay clubs" on the internet, rarely did I come across a picture of men of color. What I found were promotional flyers for clubs showing only white muscular men. This gave me the perception that only white muscular men are attractive. The reason why someone would be on a flyer or shown as the "face" of a club is because they are attractive and it is presumed that this type of person will attend that club. Having a club that includes nearly every taste and every race is ideal, especially for the world we live in now, a society that we want to challenge and a world that we want to make better and more accepting. We fail to realize that not only are gays struggling to get recognized and respected but even more so for the gay men of color.

In a blog post I came across, a gay man spoke about his views on why he feels white gay men are considered more attractive than gay men of color. He expresses that the reason he, personally, does not view gay men of color as being attractive is because he "blames the entertainment [he] was surrounded by as a child. The prince charming hero type was generally a white man" (Lucasvncs). So with that said, I am sure others feel the same way about white gay men. This is why that mindset needs to be broken and tested with diversity in all spaces, especially the gay clubs.

My idea of a queer utopia in regard to clubs is to just make it more accessible for everyone. Providing only one specific taste for a club in general is ridiculous, an assortment of men is quintessential for a gay club. Gay clubs are one of a kind because of the themes, events, and free-spirited feelings experienced. Gay clubs have the upper hand in achieving the exotic and vibrant factor. The only concern is that gay clubs need to encourage different races and a little something more than oily muscle men.

Works Cited

Jindal, Priyank. "Sites of Resistance or Sites of Racism?" *That's Revolting.* Ed. Matilda Bernstein Sycamore. Berkeley: Soft Skull Press, 2004. 39-41. Print.

"LGBT Stereotypes." *Algbtical.org.* The Association for Lesbian, Gay, Bisexual and Transgender Issues in Counseling of Alabama, n.d. Web. 09 Mar. 2015.

Lucasvncs. "Are Black Men Less Desired Than White Men?" *Reddit.com.* Reddit, 24 Aug. 2014. Web. 10 Mar. 2015.

RACISM CREATES BOUNDARIES
Chad Marin

Instructor: Melisa Malvin-Middleton

CRITICAL QUESTION

This author argues that racism creates social borders and bias. What rhetorical devices and organizational strategies does the author employ to support his thesis and develop the argument throughout the essay? Give examples and explain.

Author Statement: *In this argumentative essay, I chose to write about the racial discrimination toward young minorities who become trapped by borders that are set through the racism directed toward them. I chose to write about this because I can relate to the discrimination that takes place in everyday life. I feel that these young minorities are left out; therefore, awareness must be made for them. Throughout this essay, I have researched and learned many new issues concerning this type of discrimination and included it within my essay. This is an argument for the purpose of helping those who suffer these forms of discrimination every day.*

The idea that non-whites are different and therefore should be treated different is a common perception in the United States toward minorities. This racism affects many people, not just African Americans and whites, but various diverse groups as well. Throughout the discrimination of these non-white races, the ones who suffer most are the younger generations: the ones in school and the ones who will make a change in the future. These young adults face racial profiling and social inequalities, which affect their rights as citizens in the U.S. in their daily lives. In both *Always Running* by Luis J. Rodriguez and *Twilight: Los Angeles, 1992* by Anna Deavere Smith, these issues of discrimination occur throughout the lives of these minorities and affect the way they live in the U.S. Racism and discrimination are immoral by the way they degrade minority teens through the use of figurative borders, linguistics barriers, and social-bias tendencies.

Diversity of races is treated as a threat and creates the sense of not fitting into America's criteria, which constructs figurative borders. These differences separates races from American culture, which makes it difficult for these non-white races to find jobs, get security, and overall equality. In the school systems, for these teens of diverse race, they are given less opportunity and resources than that of white Americans. Discriminatory intent can be found in various schools where these minorities attend, especially in the Los Angeles area where these disparities can easily be seen. In a letter from the U.S. Department of Education, Catherine E. Lhamon mentions how "schools serving the most black and Latino students are 1.5 times more likely to employ teachers who are newest to the profession (who are on average less effective than their more experienced colleagues) as compared to schools serving the fewest of those students" (4). This form of discrimination is immoral in the sense that schools in areas where there are more Latinos and African Americans are treated as if they are not capable of fulfilling the academic standards expected from average American students or that of which white students could accomplish. This is just one of the rising issues that occurs through these young minorities' lives that leads to many issues.

The minorities are subjected to figurative borders in the U.S., whether they are born in America or if they actually immigrated here. This portrays how the minorities are not truly free to live their dream peacefully. The students in schools get treated half-heartedly and are looked upon as if they have no potential. This leads the young minorities to slack off and be involved with those who have dropped out and are in gangs. This restriction of acceptance is the main downfall of these minorities especially as shown in *Always Running*. For example, Luis Rodriguez explains how this separation has forced his people to fight against each other through gang-related scenarios, committing crimes that set them back. Anna Deavere Smith's perspectives in her novel show how this separation can lead to tension against others and lead to misunderstandings as a whole. The racism initiates the tension and again makes it difficult for other races to truly live the American dream.

Issues containing figurative borders are immoral in the long run. This form of discrimination is inhumane and should not make students or teens, regardless of race, be a part of it. Being U.S. citizens, there should be no enemies, yet we make minorities threat number one. This discrimination is the insecurity this country still holds on to and releases by being biased and racist. Many of these issues can still be seen in inner-city places and schools. To begin with, fitting in American culture is difficult. Personally, I am Hispanic and have some Italian in my roots. In my family some are white, and some like me are very dark and resemble the average Mexican American. In my case, I experienced these figurative borders in my community. Although I do not speak any Spanish and had the same culture as whites when it came to holidays, sports and other involvements, I was often shunned in the eyes of my peers. Hearing the slurs being made to me didn't really make sense. They judged me and based their separation on the color of my skin. It opened my eyes to how at this point in time, where diversity is so ever changing, these issues should not occur, and by surprise they still do.

The next issue is the miscommunication from linguistic barriers. Aside from the figurative borders, linguistic barriers play a huge role in the way these minorities live in our community. In Luis J. Rodriguez's novel *Always Running*, an example of this is when Rodriguez's father is fired from his job because the students could not understand him clearly. This problem is definitely one reason it is hard to find an honest job for these minorities. The ability to communicate is important in adapting to this culture in America. Race plays a huge factor like a lot of other issues involving the education department. The fact that minorities are judged because of the way the way they speak is very immoral by how it makes minorities lose credibility.

The idea of linguistic barriers can change the way people treat a person in and even out of the schools in public. Such as when individuals try to tell officers they are innocent or even ask a question, some of these young minorities would get beaten up for no apparent reason, except because they were "different." No matter what races they were, they have often been attacked racially whether it was physically or verbally. Today there are still microaggressions from people, even young children who have never experienced these racist stereotypes first hand. The idea that these minorities are a threat and they will take our jobs is a common fear that in American history has often resulted in expressions of hate. In order to control these supposed threats with unequal rights, brutality is displayed in these inner-city areas in our community. Both novels show these issues very clear, and each has its own scenario and effect on the people near this racist discrimination. This barrier of language is difficult enough for those who speak another language. They must deal with problems from many sources, and it is hard to communicate or have an identity in America if one does not understand English in most places. Suffering from discrimination and not being taken seriously or even considered as equals is immoral.

The last issue found in both novels is the cruel brutality force that was inflicted on these minorities for not fitting in due to their differences in the ways they looked and talked. They were beaten harsher than a white person would have been. Police brutality, street bullying, and other forms of hate crimes were common during this time. In *Twilight: Los Angeles, 1992* and in *Always Running*, for example, both had situations where police would drag young minorities and take them to gang territory on purpose, even young children, and left them there with the enemy. There was no restraint, and most of these actions led to young children dying or getting seriously hurt. This was inhumane and wrong to treat another this way to prove a point because of the way someone looks or acts. Constant aggression is found throughout these times in the 1990s, and it results in more oppression. In *Twilight: Los Angeles, 1992*, this can be best seen when it came to the Rodney King beating, which was police brutality primarily due to race. This abuse led to an uprising or a riot in order to demonstrate what is right and equal. The law was so corrupt that action had to be taken, which shows how this discrimination was bad for everyone; even some innocent people were hurt.

Although, many white Americans feel that racism is not really an issue today. According to Z. Byron Wolf, 57% of white Americans do not believe racism is consistently occurring. While many of these Americans feel that there is no issue of racism within the justice system, there are still biases and inequalities that African Americans, Hispanics, and Asian Americans face. It is a serious issue that affects the lives of many minorities, those working and those in school.

Racism and discrimination play a huge role on young minorities in their academic and social lives. The two novels *Always Running* by Luis J. Rodriguez and *Twilight: Los Angeles, 1992* by Anna Deavere Smith portray how these issues come into action. The separation— due to figurative borders, miscommunication through linguistic barriers, and the cruel brutality these minorities face—is immoral and affects many of these young Americans. If there would be more awareness from the public, a better future for these minorities could be made and lead to equality and understanding among a diverse community.

Works Cited

Lhamon, Catherine E. Letter. "Dear Colleague Letter: Resource Comparability." *United States Department of Education*, 01 Oct. 2014: 01-37. Web. 27 Apr. 2015.

Rodriguez, Luis J. *Always Running: La Vida Loca, Gang Days in L.A.* Willimantic, CT: Curbstone, 1993. Print.

Smith, Anna Deavere. *Twilight: Los Angeles, 1992.* New York, NY: Dramatists Play Service, 2003. Print.

Wolf, Z. Byron. "CNN / ORC Poll Finds Racial Divide on Police, Justice System" *CNN.* Cable News Network, 22 Dec. 2014. Web. 27 Apr. 2015.

Burger King's "Rewind" and the Issue of White Normativity

Ariana Hardwick-Jones

Instructor: Anna Dawahare

Critical Question

How does this author use theories, such as W.E.B. Dubois's double consciousness, to support her analysis of a Burger King commercial? Furthermore, how does the author's evaluation of the ad's visual rhetorical help contribute to her argument? Explain.

Author Statement: *When this essay was assigned, I was completely clueless as to what I would write about. Once I found the "Rewind" Burger King commercial, I realized that it matched perfectly with a topic that I had been researching just out of personal interest last summer: white normativity. Writing this essay was the perfect opportunity for me to use both my previous knowledge of the subject and to explore it deeper. I hope that sharing my essay will bring attention to the issue of white normativity.*

A commercial called "Rewind," put out by the popular fast-food chain Burger King, presents a seemingly pleasant visual montage of a man's life, starting from childhood and going all the way to being a senior citizen, all while enjoying Burger King's famous "Whoppers" along the way. The commercial starts off with the text, "Whopper, America's favorite burger" and then continues to show various clips of the main subject, starting out as a child, continuing on to adolescence and young adulthood, then into a full grown married man with kids, and finally, an elderly man, accompanied by his now mature children. In every clip, the man is shown happily eating a Whopper, and finally, when he is an old man, he takes a big bite into Burger King's new Barbeque Bacon Whopper. The commercial may seems harmless at first, but deeper analysis of this fifteen second advertisement reveals that this commercial is using the image of a white family to sell the Barbeque Bacon Whopper because of the social construct of white normativity.

In the Burger King advertisement, the main male actor and his family are all white. This representation of the idealized white, middle-class family, that lives in a nice house and has two kids, is what is seen in our culture as normal. It is used to represent and be relatable to all Americans. However, this is not the case, and that is what leads us to the issue of white normativity. White normativity is "the normalization of whites' cultural practices, ideologies, and location within the racial hierarchy" (Emerson). In other words, the way that whites look, live, and think is just the normal way for things to be, and that anything that deviates from that is "different" or "other."

The roots of white normativity have beginnings that trace all the way back to when America was first colonized by Europeans, resulting in an overall Eurocentric culture in America. This Eurocentrism has caused white Americans to be seen as the normal, default, and neutral people. This idea is what leads to white transparency, or invisibility of "white" as a race, and instead just the natural human being, as if it were the original person, the backdrop of all people. In Richard Dyer's book, *White: Essays on Race and Culture*, he states, "As long as race is something only applied to non-white peoples . . . they/we function as a human norm. Other people are raced, we are just people," in reference to white people.

The invisibility of white normativity and white as a race has had a deep psychological effect on American society, especially people of minority races. Non-whites living in America suffer from a phenomenon, that W.E.B. Dubois identified as "double consciousness," which is the viewing of the self through the eyes of the other (qtd. in Kramer). Double consciousness in America is a result of white dominant culture and normativity taking a toll on the psyche of the non-white population. It is described as "the process of internalizing the viewpoint of the dominant culture" (Kramer). The reason why double consciousness is harmful to American non-whites is because they begin to have feelings of self-loathing and insecurity. Dubois, who originally coined the term, describes it as "measuring one's soul by the tape of a world that looks on in amused contempt and pity" (qtd. in Kramer). The reality of living in a culture where the ideal "normalness" will always be unattainable damages the minds of minorities. This situation can be compared to someone who looks up to something and simultaneously loves it and hates it because he or she wants to become it but has to face the truth that they cannot. Internalization of the dominant white culture leads to a constant reminder of the false idea that "It's better to be white" paired with the painful realization: "I am not white." For example, Ronald Hall addresses the "bleaching syndrome," which is the issue of African Americans bleaching their skin lighter in order to meet up to the internalized ideal of what an American looks like. Hall writes about "African Americans who internalize light skin and other dominant culture criteria as the ideal point of reference for full assimilation into American society." Another example of this double consciousness is the way that Asian women are getting plastic surgery to look more "Western." They get surgeries to get double eyelids and thinner, higher noses with the hope of becoming more successful in life. "The acceptance and the internalization of the Western beauty myth, as evidenced through plastic surgeries, is especially visible . . . in Asian immigrants to the West" (Kramer). Many people's rationale for getting cosmetic surgery is to deracialize themselves, or erase their race, but the entire idea of erasing one's race is based on a belief in white normativity, because it still puts the white race as being the normal and neutral. It is as if you were looking at a portrait of a non-white person, began to erase it with an eraser and under it there would be a white face instead. The analogy characterizes the way that double consciousness has caused non-white groups to believe they are not "normal" and that a white person is a basic person.

Getting back to the Burger King commercial, the white family in the commercial just reinforces the idea of white normativity. The commercial is most likely geared toward adults because it has a sense of maturity since the main actor grows to be old and has a sense of nostalgia because of the grainy camera effects and music that sounds like it came from an earlier time in America. However, what's more noticeable, is that the Burger King commercial has a narrator that says, "The taste you always loved" while showing this white male actor eating the Whopper throughout his years. So when the narrator says, "you" it is referring to both the audience and the main actor, but the main actor is white. This commercial assumes that "you" are white. Therefore, if you are not white, you're different or "other." This use of the word "you" while showing a white male on the screen just reinforces the white normativity, it makes it so that the basic person, like the lead actor, is just assumed to be white. Another thing to take notice of is the way the text in the beginning says, "Whopper, America's favorite burger." But in the commercial it shows a white male and his family doing all the "normal" white things: playing baseball as a kid, living in a house, raising a family. So what this commercial is implying is that this idealized white family represents America, which is just another addition to the white normativity; because, if people believe that this image of this family represents America, then that makes it the norm. Even though many people may not experience the lifestyle presented in the ad, the portrayal of a white family living in the stereotypical "average" way sends out the message that this is America, and this is everyone's culture.

Something to notice in the commercial is the way that the grainy quality of many of the scenes in the beginning is supposed to give off a sense of nostalgia, as if everyone's childhood was like this white man's childhood, so they can all look at this and relate to it on an emotional level. The feeling of relatability pertains to the feeling of trust. And trust is what is used to sell the burger, hence the line, "The taste you always loved." However, the advertisers are not just relying on the viewers buying into the idea that Burger King can be trusted, but they are also using the idea that "normal" is trustworthy as well. In this commercial, as in all of American culture, what's "normal" and what's "trusted" is white. The shaky camera work is meant to project authenticity, so that you feel you can trust this white man and his family because they have shaky videos of good times just like you do. The slow, country music gives the atmosphere of that "good ol' American" lifestyle; because, it could easily accompany a scene of a white family sitting on the porch of a country house and spending quality time with family. Not to mention, the narration sounds like that of a white male as well. The combination of all of these aspects of the commercial causes it to have the feel of good-natured, nostalgic, classic American atmosphere, for the intention of making the viewers feel as though they relate to it and trust it. However, of course, the presentation of the "normal" American family as being both average and trustworthy creates a white normativity, transparency, and as a result, self-loathing and double consciousness in the minds of minority races.

Within Phil Smith's writing, "Whiteness, Normal Theory, and Disability Studies," there is a quote from the poet Toni Morrison: "deep within the word 'American' is its association with race . . . American means white" (qtd. in Smith). The existence of a dominant white culture in America has a deep effect on people of minority races and casts out anyone who is non-white as being "other." Commercials like the Burger King Barbeque Bacon Burger ad only exacerbate the issues of double consciousness and the invisibility of the white race. Instead of allowing these harmful ideas to continue to exist, there should be a complete refusal of the idea of normality. America is a country of immigrants from all over the world with many different cultures and values. Even beyond culture, all human beings are different. Every individual person has different likes, dislikes, motivations, ideals, and more. There will never be a such thing as "normal" that everyone can relate to. Whenever any sort of single, normal, neutral ideal is created, it automatically leaves out someone or some group. It causes there to be alienation and feelings of "otherness" among anyone who does not fit that particular, specific mold. It also gives anyone who does fit that mold an advantage in society overall, which completely eliminates any sort of equality among all people. The creation of white normalness and transparency causes countless numbers of people and groups to feel the effects of not being normal and therefore they hurt themselves in order to achieve an ideal that they simply can never reach, an ideal that was not based around them. This leads to psychological distress on a day-to-day basis, which, if thought about, is incredibly cruel because the effort to reach the ideal "normalness" is futile.

Works Cited

Burger King. "Rewind." Commercial. Burger King, 04 Jul. 2014. Web. 09 Dec. 2014.

Dyer, Richard. *White: Essays on Race and Culture.* London: Routledge, 1997. Print.

Emerson, Michael O. "The Persistent Problem." Waco, Texas: Baylor University, 2010. PDF file.

Hall, Ronald. "The Bleaching Syndrome: African Americans' Response to Cultural Domination Vis-a-Vis Skin Color." *Journal of Black Studies* 26.2 (1995): 172-84. *SAGE Journals.* Web. 09 Dec. 2014.

Kramer, Eric Mark, ed. *The Emerging Monoculture: Assimilation and the "Model Minority."* Westport, Connecticut: Praeger, 2003. *Google Books.* Web. 09 Dec. 2014

Luu, Hien. "Eurocentrism: It Affects You, Too." *The Observer.* Notre Dame and Saint Mary's, 12 Sept. 2011. Web. 09 Dec. 2014.

Smith, Phil. "Whiteness, Normal Theory, and Disability Studies." *Disability Studies Quarterly.* The Society for Disability Studies, Spring 2004. Web. 09 Dec. 2014.